The
Combined
Gospel

Bill Kernan
Sara Whitney

The Combined Gospel
Copyright © 2009
Sara Laurell Publications
saralaurellpublications@live.com
Established 2009

SL

ISBN: 9781453662588

Bill Kernan
P.O. Box 884
Cadiz, KY 42211

Sara Whitney
P.O. Box 572
Datil, NM 87821

A special thanks to my daughter, Sara, without whose efforts I would find myself in another fine predicament. Your talents and willingness to help are greatly appreciated.

Also, many thanks to Pauline Wanek for all of your help. We greatly appreciate your love and support, you have been a wonderful friend to our family. We love you.

From the Authors

"The Combined Gospel is a simplified, easy to read account of the four Gospels; Matthew, Mark, Luke, and John. It includes all of the events in all of the Gospels, written in an orderly, easy to understand style, without much of the repetition and complexity which tends to deter many bible readers. God's word in our lives is most important and so necessary. Our hope is that the Combined Gospel will bless you in a special and personal way."

Bill Kernan

"When I felt the need to further my understanding of God, I was so overwhelmed by trying to take in the extent of the Bible. When reading through it, it was difficult for me to piece together the different information found in each of the Gospels. To be able to read through the life of Jesus in a sequential, continuous book has helped me grow a deeper understanding of God's message."

Sara Whitney

Introduction

In writing The Combined Gospel, I encountered greater challenges than had been anticipated. In comparing the details of a specific event in each of the four Gospels in which an account of that event is recorded, I found many differences; in the details of the event, in the location where it occurred, and in the order in which it occurred.

I used seven different translations and read each account in each of the Gospels in which it appears, in each of the translations; and then settled on what seemed to be a most likely scenario.

My hope is that you will find The Combined Gospel both easy and enjoyable to read.

Thank you and may the Lord Bless!

Bill Kernan

In the beginning the
Word was with God,
and He was God.
All things were created
through Him and by Him.
Apart from Him,
nothing was created.
In Him is life,
and this life gives light
to all mankind.
His light shines even
in darkness, and darkness
cannot overcome it.

John 1:1-5

Chapter 1

In the days of Herod, king of Judea, there lived a God-fearing man named Zacharias, of the priestly order of Abijah. He and his wife Elizabeth were both advanced in years, and yet had no child. When Zacharias was chosen by lot to perform the duties of priest in the temple, an angel of the Lord appeared to him.

"Don't be afraid!" The angel said, "I am Gabriel, and have been sent by God with this message for you. Your prayer has been heard. Your wife shall conceive and bear you a son, and you shall name him John. He shall bring you and many others much joy, and shall be great in the sight of the Lord. He shall drink neither wine nor other strong drink, and he shall be filled with the Holy Spirit, even from his mother's womb. He shall go before the Lord in the spirit and power of Elijah, and many in Israel shall turn to the Lord their God. His mission shall be to prepare a people ready for the Lord's arrival."

Zacharias responded, "How can this be, for my wife and I are both old?" The angel answered, "All things are possible with God, and my words are true. However, because you did not believe me, you shall not be able to speak until the child is named."

In the sixth month of Elizabeth's pregnancy, the angel Gabriel appeared to Mary, a virgin betrothed to a man named Joseph, in the Galilean town of Nazareth. He said to her, "How blessed are you and favored of

God. You shall conceive and bear a son, and you shall name Him Jesus. He shall be called the Son of the Most High, and shall save many from their sins. Of His Kingdom and His reign there shall never be an end."

Mary replied, "How will this happen since I am a virgin?" Gabriel answered, "The Holy Spirit shall come upon you, and the Holy One who is born shall be called the Son of God." Mary responded, "I am a servant of the Lord. May this happen to me as you say."

Upon Mary's being found with child, Joseph did not understand and yet did not want to disgrace her publicly, so he had it in mind to divorce her quietly. In his dream, an angel of the Lord appeared and said, "Don't be afraid to take Mary as your wife, for the child within her is conceived of the Holy Spirit. You shall name Him Jesus." So Joseph took Mary as his wife, but she remained a virgin until the child was born.

Now Mary went to visit Elizabeth, her blood relative, who was then six months pregnant. When Elizabeth heard Mary's greeting, the baby in her womb leapt for joy, and she was filled with the Holy Spirit. She said to Mary, "Blessed are you among women, and blessed is the Holy Child within you. You believed God, and these things He has told you will happen." Mary responded, "Oh how my soul praises the Lord; my heart rejoices in God my Savior. He has noticed His lowly servant girl, and now all generations will call me blessed." Mary stayed for a space of time, and then returned to Nazareth.

Soon Elizabeth gave birth to her son and, on the eighth day after, relatives and friends came to the circumcision ceremony; and to share her joy. They were going to name the child Zacharias, after his father, but his mother said, "No, he is to be called John!" They were puzzled, "But there is no one in all your family by that name." When Zacharias was asked, he wrote on a tablet, "His name is John!" At that moment, his tongue was loosed and he began to speak and to praise God. He was filled with the Holy Spirit and prophesied, "Blessed be the Lord God of Israel, for He has visited and ransomed His people. He has sent us a mighty Savior from the royal line of His servant David, just as He promised through the Prophets of long ago. Now we will be saved from our enemies and from all who hate us. He has been merciful to our ancestors by remembering His sacred promise to our father Abraham. Now we can serve God without fear, in holiness and righteousness for as long as we live."

He continued, "And you my little son, will be called a Prophet of the Most High, for you will prepare the way for the Lord's arrival. You will tell many how to find salvation through the forgiveness of their sins. By God's tender mercy, the light from heaven is about to shine upon us. It will shine on those living in darkness and in the shadow of death, and will guide us onto the path of peace."

John grew and became strong in spirit, and lived in the wilderness until he began his ministry to Israel.

Chapter 2

In those days, Caesar Augustus decreed that a census should be taken throughout the land, and all went to their own towns to be registered. Joseph, being a descendent of King David, went to Bethlehem [David's ancient home] with his betrothed wife who was near her time of delivery. While they were there the child was born, and because there was no room for them at the Inn where travelers lodged, Mary wrapped Him in strips of cloth and laid Him in a manger. There were shepherds in the fields nearby, keeping watch over their flocks of sheep.

It was night when an angel appeared among them, and the glory of the Lord shown around them. "Don't be afraid!" The angel said, "I bring you Good News. Today in the town of David, a Savior has been born! He is the Messiah and Lord. You shall find Him wrapped in cloth and laid in a manger." A vast host of angels joined in praise to God proclaiming, "Glory to God in the Highest, and peace on earth to those on whom His favor rests."

When they were alone again, the shepherds decided, "Let's go to Bethlehem and see this wonderful event which the angels have made known to us." They left in haste, and found Joseph and Mary with their newborn baby, which Mary had laid in a manger. When they had seen Him, they joyfully spread the word concerning all that had been told to them about this child, and all who heard it were amazed. Eight days later the child was circumcised, and He was given the name Jesus.

Having returned to Nazareth, when the days of Mary's purification were completed, Joseph and Mary took Jesus to the temple in Jerusalem to dedicate Him to God, and to offer a sacrifice of a pair of doves or two young pigeons; according to the Law of Moses.

In the temple, there was a man named Simeon, righteous and devout, who was ever awaiting the promised Messiah of Israel; for the Holy Spirit had revealed to him that he would not die before he had seen the Lord's Christ. When he saw Jesus, he took Him in his arms and prayed, "Father in heaven, You can now dismiss Your servant in peace; You have fulfilled Your word. My eyes have seen Your salvation which You have prepared in the sight of all people; a light for revelation to the Gentiles, and for glory to Your people Israel." Then Simeon blessed them and said to Mary, "This child is destined to cause many in Israel to fall. He will be rejected by many, but many others will be overcome with joy, and the deepest thoughts of men's hearts will be revealed. Even your own heart will be pierced, as though with a sword."

Also in the temple was Anna, a widow and Prophetess, who served God always in prayer and fasting. Upon seeing Jesus, she gave thanks to God, and spoke of the child to all who were yearning for the coming of the promised Messiah.

When the requirements of the Law had been fulfilled, the family returned to Nazareth. About this time, wise men from the east came to Jerusalem and asked, "Where is the one who has been born King of the Jews? We saw His star and have come to worship Him." When Herod heard of this inquiry, he was greatly disturbed, and called together the chief priests and teachers of the Law to ask them where this King was to be born. They replied, "In Bethlehem of Judea, for the prophet wrote, 'But you Bethlehem, in the land of Judah, are not the least among the princes of Judah. For out of you shall come a Ruler who will shepherd My people Israel." Herod then called in the wise men, and determined from them the exact time the star had first appeared. He told them, "Go to Bethlehem and search carefully for the child, and when you have found Him, bring word back to me so that I may go and worship Him too."

The wise men followed the star, which had led them from the east, until it stood over the place where the young child was. Filled with joy, they entered the house where mother and child were, and bowed down and worshipped Him. They presented gifts of gold and incense and myrrh to Him. Then, having been warned in a dream not to return to Herod, they departed to their own country by another way.

An angel appeared to Joseph in his dream and said, "Arise, take the child and His mother and flee to Egypt. Herod is going to search for Him to kill Him. Stay in Egypt until I tell you to return."

When Herod saw that he had been deceived by the wise men, he became violently angry and gave orders to kill all the male children in Bethlehem and all its districts, from two years old and under;

according to the time he had determined from the wise men. Thus was fulfilled that which was spoken by the Prophet Jeremiah, "A cry was heard in Ramah; a deep and painful sadness, for Rachael was weeping for her children; unable to be comforted because they are no more."

Chapter 3

Now when Herod had died, an angel came again to Joseph in a dream and said, "Arise, take the child and His mother home to Israel, for he who sought His life is dead." On the journey home, Joseph learned that Archelaus, Herod's son, was now king of Judea and he was afraid to go there. Upon being warned in a dream, he turned aside to the land of Galilee, and dwelt again in the town of Nazareth. And so was fulfilled what the Prophet had said, "He will be called a Nazarene."

The child grew and became strong in spirit, filled with wisdom, and the grace of God was upon Him. Each year, Jesus went with His parents to Jerusalem for the Feast of Passover; according to the custom.

When He was twelve years old, and the feast was over, His parents were traveling home but He had stayed behind in Jerusalem. Joseph and Mary, thinking He was with the others in the company, journeyed on for a day. When they couldn't find Him among friends and relatives by that evening, they went back to Jerusalem and, on the third day, found Him in the temple courts. He was both listening to and asking questions of the teachers, and all who heard Him were amazed at His understanding and His wisdom.

Mary said to Him, "Son, why have You done this, for Your father and I have been searching frantically for You?" Jesus replied, "Why were you searching for Me? Didn't you know that I had to be in My Father's house?" He returned home with them, and was obedient to them.

In the fifteenth year of the reign of Tiberius Caesar [Pontius Pilate being governor of Judea], the word of God came to John the son of Zacharias, in the wilderness.

John went into all the country around Jordan, preaching a baptism of repentance for the forgiveness of sins. The Prophet Isaiah had spoken of him when he said, "Hear the voice of one crying in the wilderness, prepare the way of the Lord. The valleys will be filled and the hills made low. The crooked paths will be made straight and the rough places made smooth. Then all flesh shall see the salvation of God."

John's clothes were made of camel's hair, and he wore a leather belt around his waist. His food was locusts and wild honey. People from Jerusalem, and all Judea, and the entire region around the Jordan River came out to see him, and to hear his message. Upon confessing their sins, John baptized them in the Jordan. Some came with unrepentant hearts. To them he said, "Brood of snakes! Who warned you to flee from the wrath to come? Let the way you live prove that you have repented and turned to God. To say you are descended from Abraham is not enough, for even out of these stones you're walking on, God is able to raise up children to Abraham." Some people asked, "What should we do then?" John answered, "If you have two coats, give one to someone who has none. If you have food, share with those who are hungry."

Tax collectors who had come said, "And what should we do then?" John replied, "Show your honesty by collecting no more than you are required to." Soldiers asked, "And what should we do?" To them he said, "Don't extort money and don't accuse anyone falsely; be content with your wages."

John continued, "I baptize those who repent of their sins and turn to God in water, but the One who comes after me is vastly greater than I am. He will baptize you in the Holy Spirit and in fire. His winnowing fork is in His hand. He will separate the grain from the chaff. The grain He will gather into His barn, but the chaff He will burn in unquenchable fire."

John used many such warnings in speaking to the people.

[In a future time, John would be locked in prison because he would rebuke Herod for taking his brother's wife and for many other wrongs.]

Now Jesus came from Galilee to be baptized by John. But John resisted saying, "It is I who needs to be baptized by You, yet You come to me?" Jesus replied, "Permit it now, for we must do what is right."

As Jesus came up out of the water, heaven was opened, and the spirit of God descended as a dove and hovered over Him. A voice from above said, "This is My beloved Son, in whom I am well pleased."

Then the Spirit led Jesus into the wilderness to be tempted by Satan. Forty days and forty nights He ate nothing, and was hungry. The Tempter came and said, "If You are the Son of God, command these stones to become loaves of bread."

Jesus responded, "It is written; man does not live on bread alone but also on every word that comes from the mouth of God." Then Satan took Him to the pinnacle of the temple and said, "If You really are the Son of God, throw Yourself down, for it is written; He will give His angels charge over You. In their hands they will lift You up, lest You strike Your foot against a stone."

Jesus replied, "It is also written; You must not test the Lord your God."

Last of all, Satan took Him to a mountain top and showed Him all the kingdoms of the world, and all their glory. He said, "All this has been given to me, and I will give it all to You, if You will bow down and worship me." Jesus rebuked him, "Leave Me Devil, for it is written; You shall worship the Lord your God and Him only shall you serve."

Chapter 4

Then Jesus returned to Galilee, filled with the power of the Holy Spirit. News of Him spread quickly throughout the whole region. On Sabbath days He was in the synagogues, teaching and reading from the Prophets. From Isaiah He read, "The Spirit of the Lord is upon Me, for He has appointed Me to bring Good News to the poor. He has sent Me to set the captives free, and to heal the broken hearted. The blind shall see, and the oppressed shall know freedom, for the time of the Lord's favor has come." As He closed the scroll He said, "The words you have just heard have been fulfilled this very day."

The people were amazed and asked, "How can this be, isn't this Joseph's son?" Jesus answered, "In time you will say, 'Physician, heal Yourself. Do here in Your own home town the same kinds of things You did in Capernaum.' The truth is that no Prophet is accepted in his home town. There were many widows in Israel during Elijah's time, in the days of famine and no rain for three and a half years, but he was sent only to a widow of Zarephath; a foreigner. There were also many lepers in the time of Elisha, but only Naaman; a Syrian, was healed."

Those in the synagogue grew violent and intended to take Jesus to the edge of the cliff on which the town was built and throw Him over, but He passed through their midst and walked away.

From then on He began to preach, "Repent, for the Kingdom of God is come." He left Nazareth and went to Capernaum.

One day while preaching on the shore of the Sea of Galilee, the people crowded in on all sides to hear Him speak. Jesus noticed an empty boat and asked the owner, Simon [called Peter], to take Him out onto the water a short way, and from there He taught the people.

When He had finished speaking He said to Peter, "Put out into deeper water, and let down your nets for a catch." Peter responded, "Master, we have worked all night and have caught nothing. Even so, because You say, we will try again." Peter and Andrew let down their nets, and this time the catch was so great the nets were in danger of breaking. They called to their partners, James and John, and together they filled both boats.

All were astonished at the catch, and Jesus said to them, "Don't be afraid! From now on you will be fishers of men." When they brought their boats to land, they left everything and followed Him.

Later Jesus found Philip, from Bethsaida, and Philip found Nathanael, and they followed Him. He saw Levi, a tax collector sitting at his booth and said, "Follow Me!" Levi left all and followed.

Now Levi hosted a banquet for Jesus in his home, and invited other tax collectors and their friends. The Scribes and Pharisees who saw this complained, "Why do You eat and drink with tax collectors and sinners?" He answered, "Those who are healthy don't need a physician, but those who are sick do. I have come to call sinners, not the righteous, to repentance." They responded, "John's disciples often fast and pray, and so do the disciples of the Pharisees, but Yours are eating and drinking." He replied, "Can you make the guests of the bridegroom fast while he is with them? However, the bridegroom will in time be taken away from them; then they will fast."

Chapter 5

Now the twelve called to be Apostles were these: Simon [called Peter], his brother Andrew, the brothers James and John who were sons of Zebedee, Phillip and Nathanael [called Bartholomew], Thomas and Levi [called Matthew], Simon the Zealot, James the son of Alphaeus, Judas who was the son of James, and Judas Iscariot; the one who would betray the Lord.

There was a wedding in Cana of Galilee, and Jesus was there with His mother and His disciples. When the wine had run out, Mary said to her son, "They have no more wine." Jesus responded, "Why does that concern Me? My time has not yet come." Mary told the servants, "Do whatever He tells you to do."

There were six water pots nearby, each with a capacity of twenty to thirty gallons. He told the servants, "Fill the pots with water, and then dip some and take it to the master of the feast." When the host had tasted the water, which had become wine, he commented to the bridegroom, "Usually the best wine is served first, and then the less expensive, but you have saved the best until last."

Jesus taught often in the synagogues and all who heard Him were amazed, for He spoke with authority. On one occasion there was a man present who was possessed of an evil spirit, and he cried out, "Let us alone, Jesus of Nazareth! Have You come to destroy us? I know who You are; the Holy One of God."

Jesus commanded, "Quiet! Come out of him!" The demon threw the man down and left, without harming him further. Those present were astonished and asked, "Who is this, that even evil spirits obey Him?"

They left the synagogue and entered Peter's house, and found Peter's mother-in-law lying in bed with a high fever. Jesus took her by the hand and as she sat up, the fever left, and she began to wait on them.

Many who were sick and maimed and demon possessed gathered outside the house, and He healed them all. Some men came carrying a paralytic. When they couldn't get near the Lord because of the multitude, they opened the roof above where He stood, and lowered the mat on which the paralytic lay. When Jesus saw their faith He said to the man, "Son, your sins are forgiven you."

Some of the scribes who were present complained, "Why does He blaspheme like that? Who can forgive sins but God alone?" Jesus knew their thoughts and asked, "Which is easier, to say your sins are forgiven or to say take up your mat and walk?" But to show them that He has authority on earth to forgive sins, He had said to the paralytic, "Arise and walk!"

One Sabbath day, as Jesus and His disciples were walking through the wheat fields, they picked heads of grain and rubbed the husks off and ate them. Some Pharisees saw this and asked, "Why do they do what is not lawful to do on the Sabbath?" He answered, "Haven't you read what David and those who were with him did, on the Sabbath, when they were hungry? David entered the House of God and brought out the consecrated bread, which is lawful only for the priests to eat, and they ate it. The Sabbath was made for man, not man for the Sabbath. The Son of Man is Lord, even of the Sabbath."

There was a man in the synagogue with a withered hand. The Scribes and Pharisees watched closely to see if Jesus would heal him on the Sabbath, so that they might accuse Him. He knew their thoughts and called to the man, "Come here!" Then He asked the teachers of the Law, "Is it lawful to do good on the Sabbath, or to do evil; to save life or to destroy it?" He said to the man, "Stretch out your hand!" and the hand was made whole.

Nicodemus, a ruler of the Jews and a Pharisee, came to Jesus by night and said, "Rabbi, we know that You have come from God to teach us, for the miracles You do prove it." Jesus said to him, "I tell you in truth, unless you are born again, you cannot see the Kingdom of God." Nicodemus was puzzled. "What do You mean? If a man is already old, how can he go back into his mother's womb and be born again?"

Jesus answered, "You must be born of the water and also of the Holy Spirit. Flesh can only reproduce more flesh, but the Spirit gives birth to new life from above."

Nicodemus asked, "How can these things be?"

Jesus replied, "You are a respected Jewish

leader, and yet you don't understand this? We speak of what we know and have seen, but you don't accept what we say. If you won't even believe what I tell you about earthly things, how can you possibly believe what I tell you about heavenly things? No one has ever gone to heaven, and returned again, except the Son of Man. He has come down and will return back to heaven again. Just as Moses lifted up the bronze snake on a pole in the wilderness, even so the Son of Man must be lifted up, so that all who will believe in Him should not be lost, but will have eternal life. For God so loved the world that He gave His only Son, that all who trust in Him may have everlasting life. God sent His Son, not to condemn people, but to save them through Him. Those who believe and trust in Him will be saved, but those who refuse to believe are already condemned. And the condemnation is this: that the light from heaven has come into the world, but men loved darkness more than light because their hearts are ever intent on evil."

Chapter 6

And so the multitudes grew, the healings were many, and many were delivered of demon possession.

In response to the wonderful miracles being performed by Jesus, the self-righteous teachers of religious Law could only say, "He is possessed of Satan! How else could He have such power to even cast out demons?" Jesus replied with, "How can Satan cast out Satan? If a kingdom is divided against itself, that kingdom cannot stand. A house divided against itself will not survive. And if Satan has risen up against himself, he will soon have an end. No one can enter a strong man's house, to plunder his possessions, unless he first binds the strong man. Only then can the house be robbed. I assure you that any sin can be forgiven, even that which is committed against the Son of Man. But whoever continues to blaspheme against the Holy Spirit will never be forgiven; it is an eternal sin." Jesus told them this because they had said He was possessed by an evil spirit.

Then His mother and His brothers came and stood outside, calling for Him. Someone said, "Your mother and Your brothers are outside asking for You." He replied, "Who are My mother and My brothers?" Glancing at all those around Him, He said, "These who do the will of God are My mother and My brothers and My sisters."

He taught them saying, "Because you are My followers, be happy when people mock and insult you and lie about you, for you have great rewards in heaven. Remember, even the Prophets before you were treated in the same way. To those who are willing to listen, I say love your enemies. Do good to those who hate you and spitefully use you. If someone slaps you on one cheek, turn the other one to him also. Give to those who ask of you, not expecting to receive anything back. Do to others as you would want them to do to you. But if you love only those who love you, of what credit is that? Or if you do good only to those who do good to you, or lend only to those you know can repay, of what credit is that to you, for even sinners do these things. If you refrain from judging, you also will not be judged. If you forgive others, you too will be forgiven. Give freely, and you will be blessed."

When Jesus had finished teaching, a leper came and knelt before Him saying, "Lord, if You are willing, You can make me clean." Moved with compassion, He reached out and touched the man and said, "I am willing, be clean." Immediately the leper was clean, and Jesus told him, "Tell this to no one, but go show yourself to the priest, and offer the sacrifice that Moses commanded for your cleansing; as a testimony to them."

When Jesus entered Capernaum, a Roman officer pleaded with Him, "Lord, my young servant lies in bed paralyzed and suffering unbearable pain." Jesus said, "I will come and heal him." The officer replied, "I am not worthy that You should enter my house, but if You just speak the word, it will happen. I know this because I too am a man under authority, with soldiers under me. I tell this one 'Come', and he does. I say to that one 'Go', and he does. To my servant I say 'Do this', and he does it."

Jesus marveled at the man's faith, and said to those around Him, "Many of the Gentiles will come from all over, and will sit with Abraham, with Isaac, and with Jacob in the Kingdom of Heaven. But many of those for whom the Kingdom was prepared, will be cast into outer darkness, where there will be weeping and gnashing of teeth." The Roman officer returned home to find his servant completely healed.

A large crowd followed Jesus. As they drew near the gate of a village called Nain, they were met by a funeral procession. The young man who had died was the only son of a widow. Jesus felt her grief and said to her, "Don't cry!" Those carrying the coffin stopped, and as He touched it He said, "Young man, I say to you, get up!" The boy sat up and began to talk, and Jesus gave him back to his mother.

The crowd was astonished and began praising God declaring, "A great Prophet is among us! We have seen His hand at work today."

Sometimes Jesus just needed to be alone, so He would go off by Himself to pray, "Thank You Father, that You have hidden certain truths from those who think themselves so wise and clever, and have revealed them instead to those who come like little children, for this pleases You."

Often He would give an invitation to the people, "Come to Me, all you who are tired and heavily burdened, and I will refresh you. Accept My teachings, for I am gentle and humble in heart, and your souls will find rest. All things have been given to Me by My Father. No one truly knows the Son except the Father, and no one knows the Father except the Son, and those to whom the Son chooses to reveal Him. Come and learn from Me, and get to know Me, for My yoke is easy and My burden is light."

Chapter 7

Now John the Baptist heard of all the miraculous works Jesus was performing, so he sent some disciples to Him to ask, "Are You the One we've been waiting for, or should we expect another?"

Jesus told them, "Go back to John and tell him; the blind see and the lame walk; the lepers are cleansed and the deaf hear; the dead are raised to life again and the Good News is being preached to the poor. Blessed is the one who does not fall away because of Me."

When John's disciples had departed, Jesus spoke to the multitude, "What did you go out to see? A weakened reed moved about by every breath of wind. Did you go out to see a man dressed in royal garments? Those men live in the King's houses, not in the wilderness. You went out to see a Prophet. I tell you, even more than a Prophet. This is the one of whom it was written, 'I will send My messenger ahead of You; he will prepare Your way before You.' The truth is, among those born of women, there is none greater than John the Baptist. Yet, he who is least in the Kingdom of Heaven is greater than John."

When those present heard these words, even the tax collectors who had been baptized by John agreed that this teaching was right, but the Scribes and Pharisees rejected it, for they had refused to be baptized by John.

Jesus said, "What can I compare the men of this

generation to? They are like children playing games in the market place. They complain to their families, 'We played wedding songs for you, and you didn't dance. We sang funeral hymns, and you didn't mourn.' If you are willing to accept it, John is Elijah, who the scriptures say is to come. For he came neither eating nor drinking and you say, 'He has a demon!' But the Son of Man has come eating and drinking and you say, 'Oh look, a glutton and a drunkard; a friend of tax collectors and sinners.' God's wisdom is proven by all who will accept it."

When John's disciples had returned and reported all that they had learned, he said to them, "You heard me say that I am not the Christ, but that I have been sent before Him. And now He must increase while I must decrease. Those who believe in Him will have everlasting life. But those who refuse Him will feel the wrath of God."

A Pharisee named Simon invited Jesus and His disciples to have supper with him. They accepted and went to his home, and sat down to eat.

A woman who had led a sinful life learned that He was there, and came into the house carrying a jar of expensive perfume. She knelt by Him, weeping. Her tears fell on His feet, and she dried them with her hair. She kissed His feet and anointed Him with the fragrant perfume.

When Simon saw this he said, "If You were a Prophet, You would know what kind of woman this is, for she is a sinner."

Jesus responded, "Simon, I have something to

say to you."

"Say it Teacher!" Simon answered.

Jesus proceeded, "A man loaned money to two people; five hundred pieces of silver to one, and fifty pieces to the other. Neither could pay him back, so in kindness, he forgave both debts. Tell Me, which one of them will love him more?"

Simon replied, "I suppose the one to whom he forgave the most."

Jesus said, "You are correct. Now look at this woman. I came into your house and you gave Me no water to wash My feet, but she has wet them with her tears and dried them with her hair. You did not give Me the customary kiss of greeting, but she has not stopped kissing My feet since she came in. You didn't even offer cheap oil for My head, [and this is a common courtesy], but she has anointed Me with expensive perfume. Therefore, her many sins are forgiven her, for she has loved much. But the one, who has been forgiven little, also loves only a little."

He said to the woman, "Go in peace, your faith has saved you."

Now Judas Iscariot carried the money purse for the disciples, and was quite agitated by this whole event. He complained, "This perfume was worth a year's wages. It should have been sold and the money given to the poor."

Jesus rebuked him, "Leave her alone! She did this in preparation for My burial. You will always have the poor with you, but you will not always have Me. The truth is, wherever the Good News is preached throughout the whole world, this woman's deed will be remembered."

Chapter 8

Jesus and His disciples traveled through towns and villages and cities, proclaiming the Good News of the Kingdom of God.

Some women accompanied them, helping to support them by contributing of their own means. Among these were Mary Magdalene, from whom seven demons had been cast out, also Joanna the wife of Chuza, Herod's business manager, and Susanna.

On one occasion while crossing to the other side of the lake, a violent storm arose, placing the boat in danger of capsizing. Jesus had fallen asleep and the disciples were terrified.

They yelled to Him, "Master, the boat is sinking; we're going to drown!"

He awoke and spoke to the storm, "Peace, be still!" and all became calm.

He said to them, "Why are you so fearful? Don't you have any faith?"

The disciples responded in amazement, "Who is this that even the winds and waves obey Him?"

When they were across the lake, they docked in the region of the Gadarenes, across from Galilee.

As Jesus stepped out of the boat, a demon possessed man met Him who was homeless and naked, and had dwelt among the burial caves for a long time.

The man had unnatural strength, and even though he was often put in chains and shackles, when the spirits would take control, he would snap the chains and smash the shackles; and run about crazy, cutting himself with sharp stones.

He screamed, "What do You want with me, Jesus, Son of God Most High? I beg You, don't torture me."

Jesus commanded, "What is your name?"

The demon answered, "Legion, for we are many." The demons begged not to be sent into eternal darkness, but rather, into a herd of about two thousand swine that were feeding nearby. Jesus allowed this, and the entire herd ran violently down the hill and into the lake where they drowned.

When the herdsmen saw this, they fled into the town and told of the incident. The towns people came out to see what had happened and found the man who had been possessed clothed, and in his right mind, sitting at the feet of Jesus. The crowd feared, and pleaded with Him to go away and leave them alone.

The man who was healed begged to go with Him.

The Lord told him, "No! Go home to your people and tell them what God has done for you, and of the mercy He has shown to you today."

When they had returned to the other side of the lake, a leader in the synagogue whose name was Jairus met them. He knelt before Jesus pleading, "Lord, my little daughter is lying at the door of death. But I know that if You will come and only touch her, she will live."

As they began to go, a woman who had been sick for twelve years with constant bleeding, came from behind and touched the edge of the Lord's garment; for she had thought, "If I can just touch His robe, I will be healed." She had suffered much at the hands of physicians, had spent all she had, and yet had not been healed.

As soon as she touched Him, the bleeding stopped.

Jesus turned and asked, "Who touched Me?"

Peter answered, "Master, the crowd is pressing against You, and You ask who touched You?"

Jesus responded, "Someone deliberately touched Me, for I felt healing power go out from Me."

When the woman realized that He knew, she confessed all.

He said to her, "Daughter, go in peace, your faith has made you well."

While He was still speaking, someone came to Jairus and told him, "Your daughter has died. There is no need to trouble the Teacher now."

Jesus said to Jairus, "Don't doubt! Just trust Me and she will live again."

When they arrived at the house, He entered along with Peter, and James and John, and the little girl's parents.

He told the mourners "Don't cry! She's just sleeping." They laughed inwardly, for they knew she had died.

Jesus went to her, took her hand and said, "My child,

wake up!" At that moment her spirit returned and she stood up. Her parents were overwhelmed with joy when she asked for something to eat.

When they left the house, two blind men followed behind calling out, "Have mercy on us Son of David!"

Jesus asked them, "Do you believe that I can make you see again?"

"Yes Lord, we do!" They answered. He then touched their eyes and said, "According to your faith, your sight is given back to you." Healing was instant.

Chapter 9

Jesus traveled everywhere, teaching in the synagogues and announcing the Good News of God's Kingdom. Wherever He went, He healed all kinds of sickness and diseases, and delivered many from their devils.

A demon possessed man who couldn't speak was brought to Him, and when He had cast the demon out, the mute spoke.

The crowds were large and seemed confused and helpless, like sheep without a shepherd, and He felt compassion for them.

He said to His disciples, "The harvest is great, but there are so few workers. Pray to the Lord, who owns the harvest, to send more workers into the fields."

They returned to Nazareth, and on the next

Sabbath, Jesus was in the synagogue teaching. Those who heard Him were amazed and exclaimed, "Where did this man get this wisdom, and how can He do the incredible things He does? Isn't He just a carpenter, the son of Joseph and Mary? And His brothers and sisters are right here among us."

He could see they were confused and said to them, "A Prophet is honored everywhere except in his home town; among his own friends and neighbors." He could not do many miracles there because of their indifference and lack of faith.

Jesus equipped the twelve with power to cast out demons, and to heal every kind of sickness and disease. Then He sent them out, two by two, with these instructions: "Don't go to the Gentiles, or to the Samaritans, but only to the lost sheep of the house of Israel. Tell them the Kingdom of God is near. See, I have freely given you authority over evil. As freely as you have received, freely give. You won't need to take along money, or a traveler's bag with extra clothes and sandals. Accept hospitality graciously, for the worker is worthy of his keep. When you enter a city or village, search for a worthy person and stay at his house until you leave town. If a community will not welcome you or listen to your words, shake the very dust off your feet as you leave there, as a testimony against them. Sodom and Gomorrah will fare better on Judgment Day than those people. I am sending you out as sheep among wolves. Be as clever as snakes, but as gentle as doves. When you are arrested, and you will be, don't worry about what you should say.

Your Father in heaven will give you the right words at the right time. All nations will hate you because you follow Me, but those who endure to the end will be saved. If you profess Me before men on earth, I will own you before My Father in heaven. But those who refuse Me here, I will also refuse before My Father there."

When King Herod heard the reports about Jesus, he said to his attendants, "This must be John the Baptizer, who I beheaded, come back to life again. That is how He can do these miracles."

The occasion for John's execution was this: Herod had taken his brother Philip's wife, Herodias, and John had told him, "It is not lawful for you to take her." She got angry and demanded that John be bound and thrown in prison. She wanted him dead, but Herod respected John and protected him because he considered him to be a good and holy man.

Herod became disturbed whenever he talked to John, but even so, he liked to listen to him.

Herod's birthday came, and he hosted a banquet for his officials and the leading citizens of Galilee. His stepdaughter, also named Herodias, came in and danced for them. The guests were greatly pleased, and Herod swore to her, "Ask me for anything you want and I will give it to you; up to as much as half of my kingdom."

The girl went out and said to her mother, "What should I ask for?" Her mother replied, "Ask for the head of John the Baptizer."

She returned to the King and declared, "I want

the head of John the Baptizer, at once, on a tray."

Herod immediately regretted his oath, because he liked John. However, because he had sworn to her and all his guests had heard him, he sent to the prison and had John's head brought on a tray. They gave it to the girl who took it to her mother.

When John's disciples learned of his death, they came for his body and laid him in a tomb.

When Jesus heard, He went to a deserted place to be alone. But the crowds discovered where He was going and followed Him. A huge multitude gathered and He welcomed them, and taught them throughout the day. As evening approached, His disciples said, "This is a remote place and it's already getting late. You should send these people home, so they can go into the villages and get food for themselves."

"That won't be necessary!" He responded, "You give them something to eat."

They asked, "But how Lord? There's a lad here who has five small loaves and two fish, and that's all we have."

Jesus instructed, "Bring them to Me, and have the people sit in groups of about fifty." He took the loaves and fish, looked to heaven, and asked God's blessing on them. Then He broke the loaves and divided the fish, and handed parcels to His disciples, who in turn distributed them to the people. All ate until they were satisfied, and twelve full baskets of broken fragments were gathered up, so that none should be wasted. There were about five thousand men, plus women and children present that day.

On one occasion, while passing through a Samaritan village where Jacob's well was, Jesus stopped to rest by the well while His disciples went on into the village to buy provisions.

At about noon, a Samaritan woman came to draw water and He said to her, "Would you give Me a drink?"

The woman was surprised because Jews and Samaritans don't interact with each other. She said, "You are a Jew and I a Samaritan, why do You ask me for a drink?"

He answered, "If you only knew the gift God has for you, and who I am, you would ask of Me and I would give you living water."

She responded, "But Sir, this well is deep and You have nothing to draw with. Where would You get this living water? Are You greater than our ancestor Jacob, who drank from this well himself? How can You offer better water than this?"

He replied, "Anyone drinking of this water will be thirsty again, but whoever drinks of My water will not thirst again."

"Give me some of this water!" She exclaimed, "So that I'll never have to carry from here again."

Jesus told her, "Go and find your husband, and come back here."

"I don't have a husband," she confessed.

He said, "You speak the truth. For you have had five husbands, but the man you're living with now is not your husband."

She said, "Sir, I can see that You must be a

Prophet, so tell me, why do Jews say that Jerusalem is the only place for worship while we say it's here at Mount Gerizim, where our ancestors worshipped?"

He answered, "The time is coming when it won't matter where you worship, but rather how you worship. True worshippers will worship in spirit and in truth. God is spirit, and those who worship Him must do so in spirit and in truth."

She replied, "I know the Messiah will come, and when He does, He will explain everything to us."

Jesus declared, "I am the Messiah, and I have come!"

The woman left her water jar and ran into the village telling everyone, "Come and see a man who told me everything I've ever done. He said He is the Messiah."

The town's people quickly came out and gathered around Him.

The disciples had returned with food, and were urging Him to eat something.

He declined saying, "I have food to eat that you know nothing about. My food is to do the will of My Father who sent Me, and to finish the work which I came to finish. Do you think the work of harvesting doesn't begin until summer ends? Look around you. Vast fields of souls are already ripe and ready for harvest. You know the saying, 'One plants the seed and another gathers the harvest,' and it's true. I sent you to reap where someone else had already sowed the seed, and now you will gather the harvest."

Chapter 10

A Jewish holy day had arrived, so Jesus went to Jerusalem.

Inside the city, near the Sheepgate, was the pool of Bethesda which had five covered porches around it.

At certain times, an angel of the Lord came down and stirred up the water. Whoever stepped in first while the water was disturbed was completely healed of whatever ailment he had. Many who were sick and maimed lay in those porches, including a lame man who had come to the stirring of the water for thirty-eight years.

Jesus knew his situation and asked, "Do you want to be healed?"

"Yes," he replied, "But I have no one to help me into the water and while I'm trying to get there, someone else always steps in before me."

Jesus told him, "Stand up, and take up your mat and walk!"

Immediately the man was healed, but because it was the Sabbath, the Jewish leaders objected, "It's not lawful for you to carry your bed on this day; it's the Sabbath."

The man replied, "The one who healed me told me to pick up my mat and walk."

"Who told you that?" They demanded.

The man didn't know for Jesus had disappeared in the crowd.

Later the Lord found him in the temple and said,

"Now that you've been made well, stop sinning, lest something worse should happen to you."

The man told the Jewish leaders that it was Jesus who had healed him.

They began to harass Jesus for breaking the Sabbath laws but He told them, "My Father is always working, and I will do as He does."

This angered the Jews because He had made Himself equal to God by claiming to be His son, and they determined all the more to find a way to kill Him.

Jesus continued, "The Son can do nothing by Himself, He does only what He sees the Father doing. Did this man's healing astonish you? I say to you, you will see far greater works than this. All judgment is left to the Son, so that everyone will honor the Son just as they honor the Father. But if you refuse to honor the Son who came from the Father, then you certainly are not honoring the Father who sent Him. Those who hear My message and believe in Him who sent Me have eternal life. They have already passed from death to life. I assure you the time is coming when all those who have died will hear My voice, the voice of the Son of God, and come forth. Those who have done right will rise to eternal life. Those who have continued in sin will face judgment and condemnation."

And still He continued, "When I make claims about Myself, they aren't believed. But John the Baptist made these same claims about Me. And I have an even greater witness than John, for My Father testifies about Me. You have never heard His voice nor seen His form at any time. You do not have His message in your hearts because you refuse to believe Me, and I am the one He sent to you. You search the scriptures because you believe they give you eternal life, and yet these same scriptures testify of Me. I have come in My Father's name, and you reject Me, but if others come in their own name, you welcome them. Moses also testified of Me, but since you don't believe what he wrote, how can you believe what I tell you?"

Jesus sent His disciples on ahead of Him, while He went alone into the hills to pray.

Late at night a strong wind came up, and the boat they were in was being battered by heavy waves. As they struggled with the oars, they saw Him coming toward them, walking on the water. They gasped in terror, supposing that He was a ghost.

He said, "It's all right! Don't be afraid, it's just Me."

Peter called out, "Lord, if it's really You, tell me to come to You, walking on the water."

"Come Peter", the Lord said.

Peter climbed over the side and began walking to Jesus. But when he was distracted by the storm, he became fearful and began to sink.

"Save me, Master!" He cried. Jesus grabbed his hand and scolded, "You have so little faith. Why did you doubt Me?" When they entered the boat, the storm quickly ceased.

Later some Pharisees questioned Jesus, "Why do your disciples ignore the traditions of our elders, for they eat without performing the ritual hand washing ceremony?"

Jesus answered, "And why do you, by your traditions, violate the commandments of God? For God says, 'Honor your father and mother, and anyone who slanders father or mother will be subject to death.' But you nullify this by telling your needy parents, 'Sorry, but whatever I might have given to you, I have vowed to God.' Hypocrites! Isaiah spoke truth when he said, 'These people honor Me with their lips, but their hearts are far from Me. Their worship is in vain, for their teachings are nothing but rules made up by men."

Then Jesus said, "Listen and try to understand. It's not what goes into your mouth that defiles you, for that just enters your stomach and then is eliminated. What comes out of your mouth comes from your heart, and that is what defiles you. For from the heart comes lying and lust and greed and all sorts of other evil thoughts. Eating with unwashed hands does not defile you."

A Canaanite woman came to Jesus begging, "Lord, Son of David, have mercy on me. My little daughter has a demon and she suffers terribly."

When He didn't respond, the disciples said to Him, "Tell her to stop bothering us and leave."

He told the woman, "I was sent only to the lost sheep of the house of Israel. It isn't right to take food from the children's plates, and throw it to their dogs."

"Yes Lord!" She replied, "But even their dogs are allowed to eat the crumbs that fall from the masters table."

He said, "Woman, you have strong faith. I have healed your daughter." She returned home to find the little girl resting peacefully, and the demon gone.

A deaf man with a speech impediment was brought to Jesus, and the people begged Him to heal the man. He took the man aside so they could be alone. He put His fingers into the man's ears, touched His own tongue and then touched the man's tongue. "Be opened", He said, and instantly the man could hear perfectly and talk plainly.

On another occasion, a large crowd had gathered in a remote place and had already been with Jesus for three days, and had run out of food.

He said, "I feel for these people. If I send them home without first eating, some may faint along the way, for some have come a long distance."

The disciples responded, "But how will we find enough food for this crowd way out here?"

He asked, "Do you know if you have any food?"

"Yes," they replied, "Seven loaves and a few fish."

"Bring them to Me," He said.

He took the loaves and the fish, looked to heaven, and asked God to bless them. Then He divided them and gave to His disciples, and they gave to the people. All ate until they were satisfied, and seven large baskets of leftover pieces were gathered up. Those present that day were about four thousand men, besides woman and children.

Chapter 11

Some Jewish leaders came to Jesus, and challenged Him to prove His authority by showing them a miraculous sign in the sky.

His response was, "If the sky is red in the evening you say, 'Fair weather tomorrow'. If it is red in the morning you say, 'Foul weather today'. You know how to read the signs in the sky, but you're too blind to see the signs of the times. No sign will be given except the sign of the Prophet Jonah. For just as he was three days and three nights in the belly of the fish, so shall the Son of Man be three days and three nights in the belly of the earth."

Once while docking the boat, the disciples discovered that they had forgotten to bring any food. They began to blame each other for being so forgetful.

Jesus warned, "Be careful! Watch out for the yeast of the Pharisees." They thought they were being reprimanded for forgetting the food.

But He said, "Why do you worry about having no food? Haven't you been paying attention? Don't you remember the five thousand I fed with five loaves and two fish, or the four thousand I fed with seven loaves and a few fish? And how about all that which was left over?" Then they understood that He was actually talking about the false teaching of the Pharisees and the Sadducees.

Upon arriving at Bethsaida, some came with a blind man and pleaded with Jesus to heal him. He took the man by the hand and led him out of the village. Then He touched His own tongue with His fingers, and touched the man's eyes.

"Can you see anything?" He asked.

"Yes!" The man replied, "I can see people, but not clearly. They look like trees walking around." Jesus touched his eyes again, and his sight was completely restored.

Then He sent him away saying, "Don't go back into the village on your way home."

While walking with His disciples Jesus asked, "Who do people say that I am?" They answered, "Some say John the Baptist, and others say Elijah or one of the other Prophets."

"But who do you say that I am?" Jesus questioned.

Peter answered, "You are the Messiah; the Christ from God."

Jesus told him, "You are blessed Peter. For you did not learn this from humans, but from My Father in heaven. It is on this profession of faith from you and from all who will believe, that I will build My church; and all the powers of Hell shall not stand against it. I will entrust you with the keys to the Kingdom of Heaven. Whatever you forbid on earth will be forbidden in heaven, and whatever you allow on earth will be allowed in heaven."

He began to explain to them that it was necessary for Him to go to Jerusalem, where He would suffer greatly at the hands of the religious leaders. He told them He would be killed but, on the third day, He would be raised back to life again.

Peter rebuked Him, "Never Lord, this will never happen to You!"

"Stand down Satan!" Jesus commanded, "You are trying to trip Me up and cause Me to fail. You are seeing things merely through human eyes and not from God's point of view."

He continued, "If anyone wants to side with Me, he must deny himself and pick up his cross and follow Me. If you value your life more than Me you will lose it. But if you lose your life for My sake, you will save it. What benefit would it be to the one who gains the whole world, but loses his own soul? What can be worth more than your soul? For I will come with the angels in the glory of My Father, and will judge all people, and will reward them according to their works. There are some standing right here who will not taste death before they see Me coming in My Kingdom."

A few days later, the Lord took Peter, James and John, and went up a mountain to be by themselves. As they watched, His appearance changed. His face shown like the sun, and His clothes became as white as light.

Suddenly Moses and Elijah appeared and began talking to Him. The disciples were terrified and Peter blurted out, "Lord this is good. Should I make three shelters; one for You, one for Moses, and one for Elijah?" He was in such a state of disorder, he didn't know what else to say.

While he was still speaking, a bright cloud covered them and a voice from the cloud said, "This is

My beloved Son, on whom My favor rests."

Then they were alone again, and Jesus told them, "Don't tell anyone about this until I have risen from the dead."

They asked, "Why do the Scribes say that Elijah must return before the Messiah comes?"

He answered, "The truth is, Elijah is coming to prepare everything. But I tell you, he has already come, but he wasn't recognized and they treated him miserably."

The disciples understood that He was speaking of John the Baptist.

At the base of the mountain a large crowd was waiting. A man came and knelt before Jesus, pleading, "Lord, have mercy on my son, my only one. He gets seizures and foams at the mouth. He is often thrown to the ground and suffers unbearably. I brought him to Your disciples, but they couldn't heal him."

Jesus admonished them, "How long will I have to stay with you until you can show some faith?"

"Bring him to Me!" He rebuked the demon and it left, and the boy was healed.

Later the disciples asked why they weren't able to cast the demon out.

Jesus told them, "Because your faith is so weak. If you had faith, even as small as a mustard seed, you could say to this mountain, 'Move!' and it will. Nothing would be impossible for you."

Chapter 12

While in Capernaum, the collectors of the temple tax came to Peter and asked, "Does your Master pay the required tax?"

"Yes He does!" Peter replied, and he went into the house to talk to Jesus about it.

Before he could speak, Jesus asked, "What do you think Peter? Do kings collect tax from their own sons or do they tax others?"

"They tax others!" Peter answered.

Jesus responded, "Then the sons are exempt. But so that they aren't offended, go to the lake and throw in a line. Open the mouth of the first fish you catch and you will find a coin worth twice the temple tax. Give it to them, for your tax and for Mine."

Sometimes the disciples engaged in senseless discussions concerning which of them was the greatest.

Jesus knew their thoughts, so He called a small child over to Him and said, "The greatest in the Kingdom of heaven is the one who humbles himself and becomes like this little child. Unless you do this, you will never enter the Kingdom. And if you welcome a child like this because of Me, you are welcoming both Me and My Father who sent Me. For the Kingdom belongs to such as these."

Some Pharisees came again to Jesus, to try to trap Him in His words.

"Can a man divorce his wife for just any

reason?" They asked.

He answered, "Haven't you read, that in the creation God made them male and female. That is why a man will leave his father and mother and be joined to his wife, and the two are no longer two, but one body. Therefore, what God has joined together, man must not separate."

They asked, "Then why did Moses write that a man could divorce his wife by simply giving her a certificate of divorce?"

He replied, "Moses permitted it because of the hardness of your hearts, but in the beginning it was not so."

They persisted, "Suppose there were seven brothers. The oldest married but died without an heir. Moses said that his brother must marry the widow, and raise up an heir for him. So the second brother marries her, and also dies without any children, and then the third and fourth, right through the seventh with no children. Finally the woman also dies. Whose wife will she be in the resurrection, for they all had her?"

He replied, "You don't know the scriptures. For when the dead rise, they will neither marry nor be given in marriage. They will be like the angels of God."

While on the road, a wealthy young man came to Jesus and asked, "Good Teacher, what can I do to know that I will have eternal life?"

"God alone is good!" Jesus said. "But to answer your question; you know the commandments, obey them."

The young man exclaimed, "But I have Lord, even from my youth."

Jesus told him, "There is one thing you haven't done. If you want to be perfect, go and sell all you have, and give the money to the poor. Then come and follow Me, and you will have treasure in heaven."

The young man walked away sad, for he had many valuable possessions.

Jesus addressed His followers, "How hard it is for a rich man to enter the Kingdom of Heaven. It is easier for a camel to crawl through the eye of a needle."

This surprised them and they asked, "If that is true, then who can be saved?"

He answered, "Humanly speaking, it is impossible. But with God all things are possible. I tell you, anyone who has left all for My sake will receive far more now; and in the future, eternal life. But many who would be first now, will be last then. And many who are last here will be first there."

James and John came with their mother and her request was, "Master, in Your Kingdom, allow my sons to sit in places of honor; one on Your right, and the other on Your left."

Jesus responded, "You don't know what you're asking. Are you able to drink from the bitter cup that is Mine to drink? Or can you bear the incredible suffering that is Mine to bear?"

"Yes Lord, we are able." They answered.

He replied, "You will indeed taste of My cup, and you will suffer for My sake. But the seats you request are not Mine to give. My Father has prepared them for whom He wills."

When the other ten heard this, they became indignant towards the two. So Jesus called them all together and told them, "Whoever wants to be a leader among you must first be your servant, and whoever wants to be the greatest, must first be your slave. For even I did not come to be served, but to serve; and to give My life as a ransom for many."

Two blind men were sitting beside the road. When they heard that Jesus was coming their way they began calling out, "Lord, son of David, have mercy on us!" Some told them to be quiet, but they just shouted all the louder.

Jesus stopped and asked, "What do you want Me to do for you?"

"Lord, we want to see!" They said. He touched their eyes and instantly they could see, and they followed Him.

While walking along someone said, "Master, I will follow You wherever You go."

He responded, "Foxes have dens and birds have nests, but I have no earthly place to call home."

To another He said, "Follow Me!" The man said, "I will Lord, but my father is old. First let me wait until he has died."

Jesus told him, "Let those who are dead in spirit bury their own dead."

Still another said, "I will follow You Lord, as soon as I go and say goodbye to my family."

He replied, "Anyone who begins to plow but

keeps looking back, is not fit for the Kingdom of God."

Chapter 13

Now the Lord chose seventy-two other disciples and sent them, two by two, on ahead into every town and village where He was planning to go.

He told them, "The harvest is ready, but there are so few workers. Be careful, and don't be worried about earthly things. I give you authority over sickness and demons. If a town welcomes you, eat whatever is set before you. Heal the sick and tell them about the Kingdom of God. If they won't welcome you, shake even the dust that sticks to your sandals off as you leave that town; as a testimony against them."

Later the seventy-two returned rejoicing, "Lord, even the demons obey us when we speak Your name."

Jesus said, "I saw Satan fall like lightening from heaven. I have given you power greater than all that which the enemy has. But be even happier that your names are written in heaven."

They entered a village where a woman named Martha invited Jesus into her home. Her sister Mary sat at the Lord's feet while she busied herself with meal preparations.

She complained, "Master, it seems unfair that my sister just sits here listening to You, while I do all the work."

"Martha My child," He responded, "You are

anxious about many things, but only one thing is important. Mary has chosen that which is most important, and it won't be taken away from her."

A Pharisee invited Jesus to his home for a meal. Jesus accepted, and sat at his table. It surprised the Pharisee that the Lord had not honored the ritual hand washing ceremony.

Jesus knew his thoughts and said to him, "You Pharisees are always so careful to clean the outside, but inside you are still dirty; full of greed and wickedness. Didn't God make the inside as well as the outside? Do His will and then you will be truly clean. You are so meticulous with your tithes, but you completely ignore justice and the love of God. You covet the most important seats in the synagogues, and you pride yourselves in the greetings you get in the market place. You're like concealed graves in a field. People walk over you without even being aware of the corruption they're stepping on."

A Scribe said, "Teacher, You have insulted us, too."

He responded, "Well let's talk about you expert teachers of religious Law. You crush people with unbearable religious demands and then don't even lift a finger to ease their burdens. You build tombs for the Prophets; when it was your ancestors who killed them. You show that you agree with what they did when you build these monuments. Woe to you scholars! You hide the truth from people, and you won't even accept it yourselves. You're always trying to prevent others from having a chance to believe."

As might be expected, the Scribes and Pharisees were furious, and began plotting for a way to have Jesus arrested.

Jesus encouraged His followers constantly to share the Good News, "Anyone who is not with Me is, in reality, against Me. If you won't gather with Me, then you are opposing both Me and My Father who sent Me. Listen now, when an evil spirit leaves a person, it wanders about looking for a place to rest. When it finds none, it returns to the house it left and is delighted to see it swept and clean; and very empty. Then it goes and rounds up seven other evil spirits, and they all enter that person and live there. The last condition of that poor soul is far worse than the first. I advise you to feed on the Word of God; until you're filled."

Jesus was teaching on a Sabbath day when He noticed a woman in the synagogue, who had been crippled by a demon spirit for eighteen years. She was bent over, unable to stand straight. He touched her and said, "Woman, you are healed of this infirmity." Instantly she could stand straight, and 'Oh' how she praised God.

The synagogue leader was perplexed that she had been healed on the Sabbath and said to her, "There are six days of the week for working. Come on those days to be healed, not on the Sabbath."

"Hypocrite!" Jesus rebuked him. "You work on the Sabbath. Don't you untie your ox or your donkey and lead it out to water? So why is it wrong for Me to free this woman from the bondage which Satan has had her under for eighteen years?"

On the border between Galilee and Samaria as He was entering a village, ten lepers called out to Him from a distance, "Jesus, have pity on us!" He told them, "Go and show yourselves to the priest." As they were on the way, they were healed. One, a Samarian, returned to Him, thanking Him and praising God. "Weren't there ten healed?" Jesus asked. "Where are the other nine?" To the man He said, "Go in peace! Your faith has healed you."

A Pharisee asked, "When will the Kingdom of God begin?" Jesus answered, "The Kingdom doesn't come with visible signs. You won't be able to say, 'Look, here it is!' or 'There it is!' The Kingdom of God is within you."

To His disciples He said, "The time is coming when you will yearn to be with Me, even if only for a single day. You'll hear reports that I am in the desert, or on a mountain, or somewhere else, but don't believe it. For when I come, it will be as evident as the lightening that flashes from one end of the sky to the other. But first I must suffer terribly, and be rejected by this generation. When I return it will be as it was in Noah's day. Before the flood, people ate and drank and married; life as usual, right up until Noah entered the boat and the storms came and destroyed them all. Or as in the days of Lot, when people went about business as usual, until fire and brimstone rained down and destroyed them all. On that day, the one outside the house must not go back inside to pack. The one in the field must not return to the village. Remember what happened to Lot's wife. Whoever clings to this life, will lose his life. And whoever loses his life for My sake, will save it. On that day two people will be in one bed; one will be taken, and one will be left. Two will be grinding grain; one will be taken, and the other left."

The disciples asked, "Where will they be taken?" He answered, "Just as the vultures gather where the bodies lie, so do these signs show that the end is come."

Chapter 14

As Jesus was passing through Jericho, a wealthy tax collector named Zacchaeus tried to get a look at Him but couldn't; for he was short and couldn't see over the crowd. So he ran ahead and climbed a sycamore tree thinking he could see from there.

When Jesus came by, He looked up and said, "Zacchaeus, come down, for I will be a guest at your home today." Zacchaeus was delighted and took the Lord home with him.

But the people grumbled, "That man is a notorious sinner." Zacchaeus said, "I will give half of my wealth to the poor. And if I have cheated anyone, I will pay back four times as much."

Jesus responded, "Salvation has come to this house today, for this man has shown himself to be a true son of Abraham."

Some asked, "Teacher, what does God want us

to do?"

He answered, "What God wants you to do is to believe in the One He has sent."

They said, "Show us another miracle to help us believe. After all, our ancestors ate manna in the wilderness, which Moses gave them from heaven." He replied, "Moses didn't give them that food, My Father did. And now He offers you the true bread from heaven. The One who comes down from heaven is the true bread that gives life to the world."

"Lord, give us this bread!" They said.

He responded, "I am the bread from heaven. Whoever comes to Me will never be hungry again. Whoever believes in Me will never thirst again. It is My Father's will that all who see His Son and believe in Him should have eternal life, and I will raise them up at the last day." The people began to murmur because He said, "I am the bread that has come down from heaven."

"Isn't this Joseph's son?" They asked, "Don't we know His family? So how can He say that He came down from heaven?"

Jesus continued, "Stop complaining about what I said. No one can come to Me unless the Father who sent Me draws him to Me. No one has ever seen the Father, but everyone who listens and learns from Him comes to Me. Anyone who believes in Me has eternal life, for I am the bread that gives life. Your ancestors ate manna and they all died. Anyone who eats the bread from heaven will never die. I am the bread of life, and the bread which I offer is My flesh; which I give to redeem humanity."

The people were confused, "How can He give us His flesh to eat?" Jesus answered, "Unless you eat My flesh and drink My blood, you will not have eternal life. My flesh is true food and My blood is true drink. Anyone who does this lives in Me, and I live in them. Your ancestors ate the manna and are dead, but anyone who eats this bread will live forever."

Even His disciples were distressed, "Master these are very disturbing words. How can anyone accept them?"

Jesus could see their mixed emotions and He said, "Are you offended by this? It is the Spirit alone that gives eternal life. The flesh is of no value at all. The words that I've spoken are spirit, and it's My words that give life. That is what I meant when I said that no one can come to Me unless the Father draws him."

Some of the followers found this teaching too difficult to accept, and they left off following Him. Jesus turned to the twelve and asked, "Will you also be leaving Me?" Peter answered, "Lord, we don't want to be anywhere else. You alone have the words that give eternal life, and we believe them. We know You are the Holy One of God."

Jesus was aware that the Jews were plotting to kill Him, so He avoided going to Judea. However, the feast of Tabernacles was soon approaching. His brothers urged Him to go to the festival. They said, "Go where more people can see Your miracles; You won't become famous if You keep hiding. Go prove

Yourself to the world."

He replied, "It's not right for Me to go at this time, but you go on ahead. They won't hate you, but they hate Me because I expose their sins." After His brothers left, Jesus also went, but secretly, staying out of public view. The Jewish leaders kept asking around if anyone had seen Him. There were mixed feelings about Him in the crowd, some said He was the Messiah, while others said that He was just another fraud. Partway through the festival, Jesus went into the temple to teach. Those who heard Him were surprised, and wondered how He knew so much when He had never been trained as they themselves were.

He told them, "What I teach is not of Myself, but rather from God who sent Me. Those who seek the will of My Father know that what I teach comes from Him. Moses gave you the Law, but you don't obey it. And the truth is, you want to kill Me."

"You're possessed!" They retorted, "Who wants to kill You?"

He answered, "I healed on the Sabbath, and you accused Me of working. But you work on the Sabbath; every time you circumcise a child on the eighth day, if that happens to be a Sabbath. So why condemn Me for making someone completely well on the Sabbath?"

Some of the citizens of Jerusalem questioned, "Isn't this the man our leaders want to kill? And yet there He stands, teaching publicly, and they do nothing. Is it possible that they believe He is the Messiah? But then, how could that be? We know this man and where He grew up. When the real Messiah comes, He'll just simply appear; no one will know where He came from."

Jesus called out, "Yes, you recognize Me, and you know where I was born and raised. But you don't know the One who sent Me. I know Him because I came from Him. He sent Me to you."

Many came to believe in Him. "After all," they admitted, "How could anyone do more or greater miracles than He has done."

On the last day of the festival, Jesus called to the crowds, "If anyone is thirsty, let him come to Me and drink. If you believe in Me, living water will flow from your heart." The living water He spoke of is the Holy Spirit, who would be given to believers after His resurrection.

Temple guards had been sent to arrest Jesus, but they returned empty handed. The Pharisees asked, "Why haven't you brought Him in?" They answered, "It's the words He speaks. We've never heard anyone talk like that." The Pharisees mused, "So He's fooled you too! Look around, do you see even one of us who believes in Him? This foolish crowd follows Him, but they're ignorant of the Law. Besides, there's a curse on them anyway."

Then Nicodemus, the leader who had gone secretly to talk with Jesus spoke up, "Is it lawful to convict a man before He is given a hearing?" They chided, "Are you a Galilean too? The scriptures state clearly that no Prophet will come out of Galilee."

Early next morning, Jesus was back in the

temple courts. A crowd soon gathered and He sat down and taught them. The Jewish leaders brought a woman who had been caught in the act of adultery, and forced her to stand before the crowd. They said to Him, "This woman is an adulteress, caught in the very act. The Law of Moses says to stone her to death. What do You say?"

They were trying to trap Him into saying something that they could use to accuse Him, but He bent down and began to write in the dust with His finger.

They demanded an answer.

"All right," Jesus said, "Stone her, but let the one who has never sinned throw the first stone." Then He continued writing in the dust.

One by one, her accusers quietly slipped away, until the woman stood alone before Him. He asked her, "Where are your accusers? Isn't there even one left here to judge you?"

"No one, Sir," she replied. He said, "Neither do I. Go now, and sin no more."

Chapter 15

Later Jesus taught again saying, "I am the light of the world. If you follow Me, you won't live in darkness because you will have the light that leads to life." Some Pharisees said, "You're making these claims about Yourself, therefore they cannot be considered valid." He told them, "My claims are valid, even though I make them about Myself. I know where I came from and where I'm going, but you don't. You judge by human standards, but I don't. But if I did, My judgment would be completely accurate, because I am not alone. My Father who sent Me is with Me. Your own law says that if two agree on something, their witness is true. I am one witness and My Father is the other."

"Where is your Father?" They asked. He answered, "If you would have known Me, you would have known My Father too." Jesus continued, "You are from here below, but I am from above. You are of this world, but I am not. I warn you, that unless you believe that I am who I say I am, you will die in your sins."

"Just who are You?" They demanded.

"I am the One I've always claimed to be," He replied. "When you have crucified the Messiah, then you will understand that I am He, and that I speak only what My Father has given Me to say. You are My true disciples only if you obey My teachings, and you will know the truth and the truth will make you free."

"We're not slaves!" They declared. "We're descendants of Abraham, so what do You mean by we will be made free?" He replied, "The truth is, everyone who sins is a slave to sin. A slave doesn't stay with a family forever, but a son is permanent. So if the Son makes you free, then you are free indeed. I realize that you are descended from Abraham, and yet some of you want to kill Me because you won't accept My teachings. I'm just doing what My Father tells Me to do, just like you're doing what your father tells you to do."

"Our father is Abraham!" They insisted.

"No!" Jesus responded, "If you really were Abraham's children, you would do the things he did, but he certainly would not have done the things you do. You choose to obey your real father."

"We are not illegitimate children!" They shouted, "God Himself is our real Father."

Jesus told them, "If God were your real Father, you would believe Me, for I have come from Him. Why can't you understand what I'm saying to you? Are your heads so dense that you can't even hear Me? No, your father is Satan, for you hate the truth and love to do evil just as he does. He murders and lies, and so do you. I assure you, anyone who belongs to God's family; and that doesn't include you, will gladly obey My teachings and will never die."

"Now we know you are possessed!" They shouted back, "For all the Prophets and even Abraham himself, died long ago. Do You really think You're greater than they were?" Jesus said, "You say, 'He is our Father,' but you don't even know Him. If I were to tell you that I don't know Him, then I would be as big of a liar as you are. But I do know Him, and I obey Him. Abraham looked forward to My day and he was glad when he saw Me." They exclaimed, "You're not even fifty years old yet! How could Abraham have seen You?"

Jesus answered, "The truth is, I existed before Abraham was even born." At that point, He left the angry crowd and the temple.

As they were walking along, they saw a man who was blind from birth sitting there begging. Some followers asked, "Lord, why was this man born blind. Was it because of his own sin, or maybe his parent's sins?" "Neither," Jesus replied. "He was born this way so that God's power could be shown in him."

Then He spat on the ground, made some mud with saliva, and spread it on the man's eyes. He told the man, "Now go and wash in the pool of Siloam. The blind man went and washed, and came back seeing.

Some who had seen him begging asked, "Isn't this the one who used to sit and beg?" Some said, "Yes!" But others said, "No! He only looks like him."

The beggar insisted, "I am the same man! The one called Jesus made some mud and put it on my eyes. Then He told me to go and wash in the pool of Siloam. So I did and here I am, and I can see. But I don't know where He could have gone now." They took him to the Pharisees because it was the Sabbath day, and the Pharisees wanted to know all about it. When he had told them the whole story, some said, "This Jesus is not from God because He works on the Sabbath." Others said, "But how could an ordinary person do the wonderful things that He does?"

The Pharisees reprimanded the man saying, "You should be giving glory to God, not to this sinner Jesus." He responded, "I don't know if He is a sinner or not, but I do know that I was blind, and now I see."

They demanded that he tell the whole story

again, but he said, "I already told you, didn't you listen? Do you want to hear it again so you can become His disciples too?"

They cursed at him, "You are His disciple. We are disciples of Moses. We know that God spoke to Moses, but we don't know anything about this man."

"Well now isn't that strange!" He mused, "He can heal blind eyes and yet you don't know anything about Him. If He were not from God, He couldn't have healed me, for God doesn't listen to sinners."

"You were born in sin!" They shouted, "And here you are trying to teach us!" They threw him out of the synagogue.

When Jesus heard what had happened, He found the man and asked, "Do you believe in the Messiah?"

He answered, "Show me who He is Sir, for I want to believe." "You're looking at Him; I am the Messiah!" Jesus replied.

"Lord, I believe!" The man exclaimed.
The Pharisees taunted Jesus, "If You really are the Messiah, tell us plainly." He responded, "I've already told you, more than once, but you just won't believe Me. The miracles I do in My Father's name should prove that I am the Messiah. You don't believe Me because you are not My sheep. My sheep listen to My voice, and they follow Me. My Father has given them to Me, and I give them eternal life. They will never die. My Father and I are one."

The Jewish leaders picked up stones to throw at Him but He said, "I have done many good works in My Father's name, for which of these deeds are you wanting to stone Me?"

They retorted, "Not for good works, but for blaspheming, because You have made Yourself equal to God."

Jesus said, "Know this! I am in the Father and the Father is in Me. My Father and I are one."

Chapter 16

Lazarus and his sisters, Martha and Mary, had become friends with Jesus. It was this Mary who had wet the Lord's feet with her tears and dried them with her hair, and then anointed Him with expensive perfume.

Lazarus was dying now, and his sisters sent a message to the Lord which said, "Master, the one You love is very sick." When He got the note He commented, "This sickness will not end in death. It is for the glory of God that the Son may receive glory because of it."

Even though Jesus loved Lazarus and his sisters, He stayed where He was for two more days. Then He said to His disciples, "Let's go back to Judea again."

"But Lord," they cautioned, "They just tried to kill You there! Why would You want to go back there?" He told them, "Our friend Lazarus has fallen asleep, but I am going to go and wake him up."

"But Lord," they surmised, "If he is only sleeping, he'll be all right."

Jesus spoke plainly, "Lazarus is dead. And I'm

glad I wasn't there, for this will be another occasion which will strengthen your faith. Come, let's go!"

When they arrived, they were told that Lazarus had already been in the tomb for four days. When Martha heard that Jesus had come, she went out to meet Him. She said, "Lord, if only You would have been here, my brother would not have died. But even so, I know that God will do whatever You ask Him to."

He assured her, "Lazarus will live again!" Martha replied, "I know that he will Lord; in the resurrection." Jesus said, "I am the resurrection, and the life! Those who believe in Me, even though they die, will live again. Do you believe this Martha?"

"Yes Lord!" She answered, "I believe You are the Messiah, the Son of God; the One who has come from God." Soon Mary came and sobbed, "Master, my brother would not have died if You had been here."

When Jesus saw everyone weeping, He was deeply troubled, and He also wept. "Where have you buried him?" He asked. "Come and see," they told Him.

When they reached the tomb, He suggested that the stone be rolled aside. Martha said, "Lord, he's been in there four days. Won't the decay have already begun?" Jesus responded, "Didn't I tell you that he will live again. Just believe!"

He looked to heaven and prayed, "Father, thank You for hearing Me. I know You always hear Me, but I speak it for the sake of those standing here, that they may believe that You have sent Me." Then He shouted, "Lazarus, come out!"

Then Lazarus came out, bound in grave clothes. Jesus told someone to unwrap him and let him go. Some of the Jewish leaders believed when they saw this, but others went to the Pharisees and told them what the Lord had done.

The Pharisees called the High Council together to discuss what action should be taken. "If we allow this Jesus to continue performing these miraculous signs, the whole nation will follow Him. Then the Roman army will come and destroy both our temple and our nation. Then what will we do?"

Caiaphas, the high priest, said, "Don't you people understand anything? Isn't it better for one man to die, than for a whole nation to be destroyed?" He didn't realize that he had prophesized of Jesus' death. From that time on, the leaders began to plot in earnest to put Jesus to death.

All males over a certain age, were required to go to Jerusalem for the Feast of Passover, which was about to happen. As they approached Bethphage on their way to Jerusalem, Jesus sent two of His disciples on ahead with these instructions, "As you enter the next village, you will see a donkey tied, with it's colt beside it. Bring the colt to Me. If anyone tries to prevent you, tell them the Lord needs it and they will allow you to take it."

They brought the colt and threw their garments over it for their Master to sit on. Others laid garments on the road ahead of Him, and still others cut leafy branches and spread them on the road. This was done to fulfill the prophecy, "Tell Israel, your King is coming! He is humble; riding on a donkey's colt."

As the procession moved along, people shouted, "Hosanna! Blessed is the One who comes in the name of the Lord! Hail to the King of Israel!"

The Pharisees complained, "Teacher, rebuke Your followers for saying these things."

He responded, "If My followers were to be silent, the very stones you walk on would burst into cheers."

It was just before the Passover, and Jesus entered the temple. He found merchants selling cattle and sheep and doves for sacrifices; and others exchanging money. He made a whip of ropes and drove them all out of the temple declaring, "My Father's house is not a place for buying and selling!" He cleared the temple of animals, and overturned the money tables. The Jewish leaders asked, "If You really have authority to do this, show us a sign to prove it."

"All right!" He replied, "Destroy this temple, and in three days I will raise it up again!"

The Jews scoffed, "It took forty-six years to build this temple, and You think You can rebuild it in three days?" Jesus was speaking of His body; and of His death and His resurrection.

When He came again to the temple, the elders demanded, "Who gave You the authority to do these things that You do?"

"I will answer your question, if you will first answer Mine. The baptism of John; was it from God, or was it merely human?"

They discussed among themselves, "If we say it was from God, then He will ask why we didn't believe John. But if we say it was human, the crowd will cause a riot because they considered John to be a Prophet." Finally they answered, "We don't know."

Jesus concluded, "Then I won't answer your question either."

Chapter 17

The Pharisees were always trying to trap Jesus into saying something for which they could have Him arrested. They sent some supporters, posing as honest men to question Him, "Teacher, we know that You are honest and impartial, and don't play favorites. So tell us, is it right for us to pay taxes to Rome or not?"

He saw through their scheme and said, "Show Me a Roman coin and I'll tell you." As they handed Him the coin, he asked, "Whose picture and title are stamped on it?" They replied, "Caesars!"

He told them, "Then give to Caesar what belongs to Caesar, and give to God what belongs to God."

Jesus cautioned His followers, "The Scribes and Pharisees may have the authority to tell you what the scriptures say, but they neither obey them nor practice what they teach, so don't you follow their example. They load you down with unbearable religious demands, but ignore them themselves. They act holy by wearing prayer boxes with scriptures inside on their sleeves; and their robes have extra long tassels. They love to sit at the main table at banquets, and in the seats of honor in the synagogues. They enjoy the attention and respect they get in the market places, and they cherish being called 'Rabbi'. Don't let anyone call you Rabbi, for you have only one teacher. You are all brothers and sisters in one family. And don't address anyone on earth as 'Father', for only God in heaven is your Father. Also, let no one call you 'Master', for the Messiah is your only Master. The greatest among you is the one who will be a servant to the rest. Those who exalt themselves will be humbled, and those who humble themselves will be exalted."

He continued, "How terrible it will be for those teachers of the Law who slam the door in the faces of the ones trying to enter the Kingdom of Heaven; and they won't go in themselves. They'll go far and wide to convert one person to their ways, and then make him twice as fit for Hell as they themselves are. They say that to swear an oath 'By God's temple' means nothing. But to swear by the gold in the temple is binding. Is the gold greater than the temple which sanctifies the gold? They say that to swear 'By the altar' is nothing, but to swear by the gifts on the altar is binding. Are the gifts on the altar greater than the altar which makes them sacred? When you swear by one, you are swearing by the other also. And when you swear by heaven, you are swearing by the Throne of God, and also by Him who sits on it."

Still He continued, "What sorrow awaits those blind guides, for they are careful to tithe of even the smallest part of their increase, and yet they ignore the important things; justice, mercy, and faith. They'll pick a gnat out of their drink, and then turn right around and swallow a camel. Woe to those hypocrites who are like whitewashed tombs; beautiful on the outside, but filthy on the inside, filled with greed and corruption and all sorts of impurities – dead men's bones. How awful for those who build monuments to the Prophets, which your ancestors killed, to show honor to their memories. Then they say, 'If we had lived then, we would never have killed the Prophets.' They prove that they are children of their ancestors, and they complete their sin. Jerusalem, Jerusalem, the city that kills the Prophets and stones the messengers sent by God. How often have I yearned to gather her children together, as a mother bird gathers her young under her wings, but you refused Me. And now, you will not see Me again until you say, 'Blessed is the One who comes in the name of the Lord."

As they walked along, the disciples commented on the various temple buildings. Jesus asked, "Do you see all these buildings? They will be completely destroyed, so that one stone will not be left on top of another."

"When will all this happen?" They asked, "What sign will signal Your return and the end of the world?"

Jesus told them, "Don't be fooled by anyone, for many will come claiming, 'I am the Christ!', and many people will be deceived. There will be wars and threats of wars, but don't be fearful, for these things must happen; but the end is not yet. There will be famines and earthquakes in some places, but this will be like the first birth pains when something new is about to be born. You will be arrested, and persecuted, and killed because of your commitment to Me. False prophets will appear and cause many to believe lies. Sin will run rampant everywhere and the love of many will grow cold; but those who keep their faith to the end will be saved. The Good News will be preached throughout the whole world, and then the end will come. The Prophet Daniel spoke of that sacrilegious thing which causes desecration, standing in the Holy Place. At that time, those in Judea must flee to the hills. Don't allow anything to hinder your flight, for the terror of that time will be greater than that which has ever been seen, or will ever be seen again. Unless that time is shortened, no flesh can survive. But it will be shortened, for the sake of God's chosen ones. Many false Christs will come and perform great signs and miracles to fool, if possible, even the strongest believers. Then if someone should say to you, 'The Messiah is on the mountain,' or 'in an inner room,' don't believe it; don't go. For as lightening flashes and lights up the entire sky; that's how it will be when I return. After those days the sun will grow dark, and the moon will not shed its light. Stars will fall from the sky, as the powers of the heavens are shaken. Then the sign of My coming will appear and all peoples will see Me coming with power and great glory. I will send the angels forth with a mighty trumpet blast, and they will gather My chosen ones from all over the earth. Learn a lesson from the fig tree. When its branches bud and new leaves begin to sprout, you know that summer is near. That's how it will be when you see all these things beginning to happen; you can know that My return is assured. The truth is, the generation that sees all this happening, will be the last generation. Heaven and earth will pass away, but My words will remain forever. However, no one knows the day, nor the hour when the end will be, only the Father knows. It will be like it was in Noah's time, business as usual, until the flood came and swept them all away. So keep watch, and be prepared. If I find you to be a wise and faithful servant who has done well, you will be blessed. If not, you will be banished to a place of weeping and gnashing of teeth."

Jesus stood near the money box in the temple, and watched as the rich people dropped their offerings in; some giving large amounts. Then a poor widow came and dropped in two small coins. He commented to His followers, "The truth is, this poor widow has given more than all the rest. They gave what they didn't need, but she gave all she had."

Chapter 18

Some Greeks had come to Jerusalem for the Passover celebration, and they found Philip and asked, "Sir, we want to meet Jesus." Philip and Andrew went together to ask Jesus. He said, "My time has come! The truth is, a kernel of wheat must be planted in the soil and die. If it's not, it will always be just one single seed. But its death will produce a great harvest. Those who love their lives here will lose them there. Those who surrender their lives here, will keep them there; for all eternity. If these Greeks want to be My disciples, tell them to come and follow Me. For My servants must be where I am, and My Father will honor them. Right now My soul is deeply troubled. Should I pray, 'Father, save Me from this trial!' No, for I came for this trial and to suffer. Rather I pray, 'Father, bring glory to Your name."

Then a voice spoke from heaven, "I have already brought glory to My name, and I will do it again." Some in the crowd thought it was thunder, but others said an angel had spoken.

Jesus said, "The voice was for your benefit, not mine. The time has come for Satan to be thrown down, for when I have been lifted up on the cross, I will draw all peoples to Me."

Despite all the miracles Jesus had performed, and all the wisdom He had imparted to the people, most of them still would not believe in Him.

Some of the Jewish leaders did however, but wouldn't admit it publicly because they feared being expelled from the synagogue; for they valued praise from men more than the praise of God.

Jesus shouted to the crowds, "If you believe in Me, you believe in the Father who sent Me. For if you have seen Me, you have seen Him. I came into the world to save it, and all who believe in Me will be saved. However, the very words that I speak will judge those who refuse to believe on the Day of Judgment."

It was now two days before the Passover Sabbath would begin. The Jewish leaders had been plotting how to arrest Jesus and have Him executed. They agreed that it should not be done on the Passover, for they would risk a riot by the people.

Satan had entered Judas Iscariot, and the leaders were delighted when he came to them, and offered to betray the Lord for a fee. They gave him thirty pieces of silver, and he began to watch for an opportune time to hand over his Master.

It was time to prepare the Passover meal and His disciples asked, "Lord, where do You want us to share this meal?" He instructed two of them, "Go into the city and you will meet a man carrying a pitcher of water. Follow him to the house he enters and say to the owner, 'The Teacher wants to know where the guest room is; where He can eat the Passover meal with His disciples.' He will show you a large room upstairs that is already set up. That's where you shall prepare the meal."

Evening came, and they gathered together for this last supper. Jesus stood up from the table, took off His robe and wrapped a towel around His waist, and poured water into a basin. Then He began washing the disciple's feet, and dried them with the towel. When He came to Peter, Peter protested, "No Lord, don't wash my feet!"

Jesus cautioned him, "If I don't, you can have no part with Me. You don't understand why I'm doing this now, but you will later."

"Then not just my feet," Peter responded. "But my hands and head as well."

Jesus replied, "Someone who has bathed already, needs only to wash his feet to be clean all over; and you are clean. But not all of you are clean," For He knew who would betray Him.

Then He continued, "Do you understand what I have just done for you? You call Me 'Master' and 'Lord', and you should because that's who I am. But since I, your Lord and Teacher, have been a servant to you, you ought to be servants to each other also. I did this as an example for you; follow My example."

When He was seated again, He said, "The truth is, one of you here with Me tonight will betray Me." The twelve were distressed by His words and began to ask, "Lord is it me? Am I the one?"

He answered, "It is the one to whom I give the bread after I've dipped it." He dipped a piece into the sauce and handed it to Judas Iscariot. Judas left the room to go to the Jewish leaders and Jesus said to the rest, "It is God's plan that I should die, but it would be better for the one who hands Me over if he would have never been born."

He then took some bread, gave thanks to God and broke it in pieces, and gave it to His disciples saying, "Take this and eat it. This is My body which I give for you. Do this to remember Me." He took the cup, gave thanks and said, "Each of you drink from it, for this is the cup of My blood, which represents the New Covenant between God and man. It is poured out for many for the forgiveness of sins. I will not drink wine again until I drink it new with you, in My Father's Kingdom."

On their way to the Mount of Olives, Jesus told Peter, "Satan has asked to have you, to sift you like wheat. But I've prayed for you that your faith should not fail. When you have repented and turned to Me again, strengthen your brothers."

He continued, "All of you will desert Me, for the scriptures say, 'God will strike the Shepherd, and the sheep will scatter.' But after I have risen from the dead, I will go ahead of you into Galilee and meet you there."

"No!" Peter declared, "Even if all the others desert You, I would never do that!"

Jesus corrected him, "The truth is Peter, before the rooster crows twice, you will have denied Me three times." Peter insisted, "Not even if I have to die for you, I will never deny You!"

The Lord took Peter, James, and John aside with Him and told them, "My soul is grieved to the point of death. Stay here and watch while I pray." He went a short distance, fell to His knees and prayed, "Father, I know that You could take this cup of suffering away from Me if that be Your will, but Your will is that I do drink it." He was in such agony that sweat fell like drops of blood from His face. An angel from heaven came and strengthened Him.

He returned to find the three sleeping and admonished them, "Couldn't you watch with Me for even one hour? Stay awake and pray so that you won't be overcome by temptation. For the spirit is willing, but the flesh is weak."

He went a second time and prayed in the same manner, and then returned to find them sleeping again, for they were exhausted. So He prayed a third time, then returned and said, "The time for sleep is over. Look, My betrayer comes."

Chapter 19

Jesus had spent a lot of time with His disciples, teaching them and strengthening their faith. He had said to them, "Don't be troubled! You believe in God, now trust in Me. There is plenty of room in My Father's house, and I'm going to prepare a place for you. I will come back and take you with Me, so that you can always be where I am. If this were not true, I would not have said it. I am the way, the truth and the life, and the only way to the Father is through Me. If you really know Me, then you know the Father too."

Philip responded, "Lord, show us the Father and we will be satisfied."

"Philip, I've been with you for a long time now," Jesus replied, "Don't you know yet who I am? Don't you understand that I am in the Father and the Father is in Me? If you have seen Me, then you have seen the Father, so how can you say, 'Show us the Father'. If you can't believe the words that I speak, then believe because of the works that I do. The truth is, My Father and I are one. Those who believe in Me will do even greater works than I have done, because I am leaving. What you ask in My name, I will do for you, but you must not doubt. If you love Me, obey My commandments. I will ask the Father and He will send you another Teacher, one who will never leave you; the Spirit of Truth. You know Him because He is here with you now, but soon He will live within you. I won't leave you orphans. I will come to you."

Jesus continued, "When the Holy Spirit comes, He will cause you to remember all that I've taught you, and He will continue to teach you. I am leaving you with a gift; peace of heart and mind. The peace that I give is not like the peace that the world gives. So don't be troubled or afraid. If you really love Me, you should be happy that I'm finally going home. I have loved you as My Father has loved Me, cherish that love. I have obeyed His commandments, and now you must obey Mine. My command is that you love one another, just as I have loved you. The greatest love one can show is to lay down his life for another. You didn't choose Me, I chose you, and if you will continue in My love, you will know joy to it's fullest. The world will hate you because you belong to Me, but I have chosen you out of the world. If they had never heard My words or seen My works, they would not be guilty, but now they have no excuse for their sin. Whoever hates Me also hates My Father. I've told you these things so that you won't lose your faith. The time is coming when those who kill you will think they're doing God a favor. They will do this because they have never known either My Father or Me. Now

I am going to the One who sent Me, and it's best for you that I do go, for if I don't, the Spirit won't come. I will send Him to you, and when He comes, He will guide you into all truth. He will convict the world of its sin, and of God's righteousness, and of the coming Judgment. The world's sin is that it refuses to believe in Me. Then when you see what I must suffer, it will grieve you deeply, but your grief will turn to joy when you see Me again. I came into the world from the Father, and now I leave the world and return to the Father."

After saying this, Jesus looked to heaven and prayed, "Father, My time has come. Reveal the glory of Your Son, so that He can bring glory to You. I've brought glory to You on earth by doing all that You've asked. Now bring Me into the glory that We had before the world began. My prayer is for all those who believe in Me, who belong to You. They will still be in the world. Keep them from Satan's treachery. As You have sent Me into the world, I am also sending them into the world. I pray for all those who will ever come to believe in Me, that they will be united and strong in truth. Then the world will know that I have come from You, and that I love them as much as You love Me."

Judas arrived with a contingent of Roman soldiers and a large crowd carrying weapons.

Jesus asked, "Who are you looking for?"

"Jesus of Nazareth!" They answered.

Judas approached Him and said, "Greetings Teacher", and gave Him a kiss of greeting. For the soldiers had been foretold that by this signal, they would know who they should arrest.

Jesus told them, "Do what you came to do, but let these others go."

When they grabbed Him, and His disciples realized what was happening, they cried, "Lord, should we fight?"

One of them drew a sword and slashed at the High Priests' slave, severing his right ear.

"Put the sword away!" Jesus ordered. "Those who use the sword, will die by the sword. Don't you know that I could ask My Father for thousands of angels, and they would be here instantly. But then, how would the scriptures be fulfilled?"

He touched the slave's ear and healed it.

Then He addressed the crowd, "Am I some dangerous criminal that you must come out with swords and clubs to arrest Me? Why didn't you arrest Me in the temple, for I taught there every day?"

At that time, all the disciples deserted Him and fled. The crowd took Jesus to the home of Caiaphas, the High Priest, where the Jewish leaders had gathered.

Peter followed at a distance, and eventually stayed with the guards to see what was going to happen.

Inside the chief priests and the council were trying to find witnesses who could accuse Jesus, so they could have Him put to death, but they couldn't find two who could agree.

Finally two came forward and said, "This man

said He is able to destroy our temple, and rebuild it again in three days."

The High Priest stood and declared, "Well, aren't You going to answer these charges? Did You say that or didn't You?"

Jesus remained silent.

"I demand answers!" Caiaphas shouted. "Are You the Messiah, the Son of the Most High God or aren't You?"

Jesus replied, "I am, and you will see Me sitting in the place of power at the right hand of God; and coming on the clouds of heaven."

Caiaphas was horrified and tore his garment. He shouted to the crowd, "You heard this blasphemy! We don't need any more witnesses. What is your verdict?"

"Guilty!" The crowd shouted back, "He deserves to die!"

Some blindfolded Him, and began to mock Him and spit on Him. Other struck Him with their fists and yelled out, "Prophesy, You Messiah! Who struck You that time?!"

As Peter was warming himself by the fire, a servant girl came by and looked at him closely. She said, "You were with Him, that Jesus from Nazareth."

"I don't know what you are talking about." He replied.

As he moved toward the entrance, a rooster crowed.

Someone else declared, "This man is one of those who followed Jesus!" Again, Peter denied it, "I told you, I don't know the man." Soon others said, "You must be a Galilean, for you have the same accent as they do."

Peter swore, "A curse on me if I'm lying. I don't know the man you're talking about!"

A rooster crowed a second time, and Peter remembered the words Jesus had told him, and he went out and wept bitterly.

Early in the morning, the council met again to discuss how they might convince the Roman government to sentence Jesus to death. Then they led Him away to Pilate, the Roman governor. When the realization that Jesus was actually going to be condemned to die sunk in, Judas was filled with regret, and took the money back to the chief priests and elders. He confessed, "I have sinned, for I have betrayed the blood of an innocent man."

"That's your problem," they mused. "Why should we care about your feelings?"

Judas threw the money on the floor, and went out and hung himself.

The priests picked up the money and cautioned, "It wouldn't be right to put this in the temple treasury, since it was payment for murder." After talking it over, they decided to use the money to buy a field where the clay was used by potters, and make it a burial ground for foreigners who died while visiting Jerusalem.

When the crowd arrived at the governor's headquarters, the Jews didn't go inside because that would defile them, and they wouldn't be allowed to celebrate Passover.

Pilate came out and asked, "What are you accusing this man of?" They responded, "We wouldn't have brought Him to you if He wasn't a criminal." Pilate suggested, "Why don't you just take Him away and judge Him by your own laws?"

They answered, "Only the Romans are permitted to execute someone."

Pilate went back inside and ordered Jesus to be brought to him.

"Are You the King of the Jews?" He asked.

"I am!" Jesus said. "I was born into the world to testify of the truth. All who love the truth know what I say is true."

Pilate responded, "What is truth?"

He went out to the crowd again and declared, "I find this man guilty of nothing!" But the Jews persisted, "But He is causing riots all over, and it all started in Galilee."

Pilate exclaimed, "Oh, so He is a Galilean then!"

When they had confirmed that He was, Pilate sent Him to Herod Antipas, who happened to be in town, because Galilee was under Herod's jurisdiction.

Chapter 20

Herod was delighted, for he had heard about Jesus, and was hoping to see Him perform a miracle. He asked question after question, but Jesus remained silent. Herod's soldiers began mocking and ridiculing Jesus. Then they sent Him back to Pilate.

Pilate called together the Jewish leaders and announced his verdict, "You have accused this man of leading a revolt. I have questioned Him and find Him innocent, and Herod agrees. This Jesus has done nothing that calls for the death penalty."

A roar of protest arose from the crowd. Now, it was the governor's custom to release one prisoner to the crowd each year at the Passover celebration.

Pilate had one in custody named Barabbas, a revolutionary who had led an uprising. The mob asked him to release a prisoner as usual.

"Do you want me to release this King of the Jews? Pilate asked.

"Not this man!" They shouted. "Release Barabbas!"

"And what should I do with this man?" Pilate asked.

"Crucify Him!" They shouted back.

"Why?" He persisted. "He's not guilty of anything!"

The crowd shouted louder, "Crucify Him, Crucify Him!"

When Pilate saw that his resistance was having no effect, and a riot was about to start, he sent for a bowl of water and washed his hands before the crowd declaring, "I am innocent of this man's blood! The responsibility is yours." They yelled back, "We take responsibility; we and our children." He released Barabbas, and had Jesus flogged with a lead tipped whip. Then the soldiers took Jesus away to be crucified.

First they took Him into the barracks, and called in the Palace Guard. They dressed Him in a purple robe and put a crown woven out of thorn branches on His head. They placed a stick in His hand for a scepter. Then they saluted and fell to their knees mocking Him, "Hail, King of the Jews." They spit on Him and took the stick from His hand, and beat Him with it. When they had tired of their sport, they dressed Him in His own clothes again and started up the hill.

Jesus was so weakened from the beatings that the soldiers compelled a man named Simon, of Cyrene, to carry the cross behind Him.

When they arrived at Golgotha, called the place of The Skull, some soldiers offered the Lord drugged wine, but He refused, for He chose to be fully conscious and of a clear mind.

Pilate had written a sign to hang on the cross. It read, "Jesus of Nazareth, King of the Jews." It was written in Hebrew and Greek and Latin to accommodate all the foreigners who were in town for the Passover celebration.

The Jewish leaders protested, "Don't write 'King of the Jews', but instead, 'This man said He was King of the Jews."

Pilate determined, "What I have written, I have written; and it stays!"

The soldiers nailed Jesus to the cross and also two criminals in similar fashion, one on His right and one on His left. When they had raised the crosses, they divided His garments between them. But His robe, being in one piece without seams, was too nice to tear apart, so they threw dice for it. This fulfilled the scripture that says, "They divided My garments among them, and for My robe they cast lots."

Jesus prayed for His executioners, "Father, forgive them, for they don't know what they're doing."

Standing near the cross were His mother and some other women, including Mary Magdalene. He said to them, "Daughters of Jerusalem, don't weep for Me, but for yourselves and for your children, for the time is coming when those who have no children will be called fortunate. Men will beg for the mountains to fall on them, and for the hills to bury them. If they do things like this when times are good, what will they do when times turn bad?"

The crowd taunted Him and shouted insults, "You saved others, why don't You save Yourself; You who can tear down our temple and rebuild it again in three days?"

One of the criminals scoffed, "Why don't You do as they say? Save Yourself, and us too while You're at it!" But the other one rebuked him, "Don't you fear God, even when you're dying? We deserve what we've been given, but this man hasn't done anything wrong."

Then he said, "Jesus, remember me when You come into Your Kingdom."

Jesus assured him, "You will be with Me in Paradise."

He saw John standing next to His mother and Jesus said to her, "Woman, there is your son." To John He said, "She is your mother." From that moment, John took her into his care.

At noon, darkness fell across the whole land. Jesus called out, "Eloi, Eloi, lema sabachthani!" which means, "My God, My God, why have You abandoned Me?"

Those who heard thought maybe He was calling for Elijah. Someone ran for a sponge and soaked it in sour wine and held it up on a stick for Him to drink. Others said, "Wait, leave Him alone. Let's see if Elijah will come and save Him."

It was preparation day for the Sabbath. This was not the normal Saturday Sabbath, but a special day; the Passover Sabbath. The Jewish leaders didn't want to leave the bodies still hanging on the Sabbath, which would begin at sunset, so they asked Pilate to hurry their deaths by breaking their legs. This was so that the bodies could be taken down and buried before sunset.

Jesus knew His work was done, but to fulfill the scripture He said "I am thirsty!" When the sour wine was held up again, He tasted it and then called out, "It is finished!" He bowed His head and released His spirit.

The soldiers came and broke the legs of the two crucified with Jesus, but when they came to Him they saw that He was already dead, so they didn't break His legs.

One soldier did however, pierce His side with a

spear, and blood and water flowed out. This happened to fulfill the scripture, "Not one of His bones will be broken, and they will look on Him whom they have pierced."

At the moment of the Lord's death, the curtain of the temple was torn from top to bottom. The earth shook, rocks split, and many tombs were laid open. Many saints who had died came back to life and, after Jesus had resurrected, they left the cemetery and went into the city where they were seen by many.

A Roman officer who had watched the execution exclaimed, "This really was the Son of God!"

Joseph of Arimathea, an honored member of the Jewish High Council and a secret disciple, went boldly to Pilate to ask permission to take Jesus' body down to be buried. Pilate granted him permission. Joseph took the Lord's body to a new tomb, which he had hewn in the rock for himself. Nicodemus, who earlier had gone to Jesus by night, brought perfume and ointment made from myrrh and aloes. Together they wrapped His body in a long sheet of linen cloth, and laid Him in the tomb. A large stone was then rolled over the entrance.

Chapter 21

The next day, on the Passover Sabbath, the chief priests and Pharisees went to Pilate and said, "Sir, we remember this deceiver telling us that He would rise back alive from the dead on the third day, so give orders to seal and guard the tomb closely until then. Otherwise His disciples might steal the body and tell everyone that He really did rise from the dead. This lie would be even worse than the first one."

Pilate responded, "Take some of your own temple police and go guard it as best you can." So they sealed the tomb and posted guards.

Sunday, the first day of the week, began at sunset on Saturday. Early on that day, Mary Magdalene and some other women were on their way to the tomb with some embalming spices which they had prepared. An earthquake had occurred and had broken the seal and caused the stone to roll away. When the guards saw this, they went to the chief priests to report what had happened. A meeting of the leaders was called and they decided to bribe the guards. They told them, "You must tell the people that His disciples came while you were asleep, and stole the body. If the governor hears of this, we'll take your side, and everything will be alright." The guards accepted the bribe and spread the story among the people.

When the women arrived at the tomb, they saw the stone rolled away and went in, but found no body.

The others left, but Mary Magdalene stayed outside the tomb, weeping. Suddenly an angel appeared in a dazzling white robe. He said to her, "Don't be afraid! I know you are looking for Jesus, but He is not here. He has risen, just as He had said He would."

As she turned to leave, another was standing

there, whom she assumed to be the gardener. She said, "Sir, if you have taken Him, please tell me where you have put Him." When the man said, "Mary," she recognized that it was Jesus immediately and screamed, "Master!" He cautioned her, "Don't touch Me! For I have not yet ascended to My Father. But go to My brothers, and tell them that I am going to My Father and your Father; My God and your God. Tell them to leave for Galilee, and I will see them there."

Two of the disciples were walking to the village of Emmaus, about seven miles from Jerusalem. As they went along, they were talking about all that had happened. Suddenly, Jesus came up alongside them and began walking with them, but they didn't recognize Him because He had a different body.

"What are you discussing so intently as you walk?" He asked.

They stopped, their faces drawn with sadness, "Are You the only person in Jerusalem who hasn't heard of all the terrible things that have happened in the last few days?"

"What things?" He asked.

"The things that happened to Jesus, the man from Nazareth," they replied. "He was a great Prophet who performed incredible miracles and spoke powerful words. But our religious leaders handed Him over to be condemned to death, and the Romans crucified Him. We had hoped that He was the Messiah who would come and rescue Israel from the Romans. This all happened a few days ago. Early today, some of our women went to the tomb, and saw that His body was missing. They said an angel had appeared, and had told them Jesus is alive. Some of our men ran out to see and, sure enough, it was just as the women had said."

Jesus said, "You are slow to believe. Wasn't it clearly prophesied that the Christ would have to suffer all these things before He would enter His glory?" Then He began to explain all that had been written about Him by Moses and all the Prophets.

When they arrived at the village, Jesus acted as if He would continue on, but they insisted, "Stay with us, for it's getting late."

So He went with them, and sat down to eat. When He took the bread, blessed and broke it, and gave it to them, they instantly knew who He was and at that moment, He disappeared. They shared how warm they had felt inside as He had talked with them, and within the hour, they were on their way back to Jerusalem.

Chapter 22

The disciples were gathered behind locked doors and the two from Emmaus were telling their story of how Jesus had walked with them, and how they knew it was Him when He broke the bread.

Suddenly, He stood right there among them, and greeted them, "Peace be with you!"

They were quite startled, and thought they were

seeing a ghost. He said, "Don't be afraid! Look at My hands and My feet. Here, touch Me and know that I am not a ghost."

Jesus asked, "Do you have anything to eat?" Someone handed Him a piece of broiled fish, and He ate it as they watched.

Then He said, "When I was with you before, I told you that everything that was written about Me by Moses and the Prophets, and in the Psalms, must be fulfilled." He opened their minds to understanding and continued, "It was written long ago that the Messiah would suffer and die, and rise to life again on the third day. It was also written that the message of the Kingdom of God would be preached to all nations. There is forgiveness of sins for all who will repent, and turn to Me. I will send the Holy Spirit, just as I promised. But stay here in the city until He comes, and fills you with power from on high."

It happened that Thomas, one of the twelve, was absent when Jesus had appeared to the others. But they told him, "We have seen the Lord!" But Thomas was skeptical, "I won't believe you unless I can see His wounds, and touch the scars."

Later Thomas was with them, again behind locked doors, for fear of the religious leaders. Jesus appeared and said, "Peace be with you!" To Thomas He said, "Here, look at My wounds, touch them, and don't doubt anymore."

Thomas exclaimed, "My Lord and my God!"

Jesus responded, "You believe because you have seen Me. Blessed are those who haven't seen Me, but still believe."

He appeared to His disciples again, beside the Sea of Galilee. Several of them were there, and Peter said, "I'm going fishing!"

"We'll all go!" The rest decided.

They fished all night, but had caught nothing. At about dawn, Jesus was standing on the shore. They could see Him, but couldn't make out who He was. Jesus called to them, "Have you brothers caught anything?'

"No!" They answered; still unaware that it was Him.

He called again, "Throw your net on the other side of the boat, and you'll get some."

They did, and this time there were so many fish, it was hard to haul the net in. John said to Peter, "It is the Lord!"

Peter jumped into the water and swam for shore, while the others stayed in the boat and dragged the net in. When they got to shore, they found fish cooking and fresh bread waiting.

"Now come and eat!" Jesus told them, and He served them breakfast.

After breakfast, He asked Peter, "Simon, son of John, do you love Me more than these?"

"Yes Lord!" Peter answered, "I do love You."

"Then feed My lambs!" Jesus replied.

He repeated the question, "Peter, do you love Me more than these?" "Lord, You know I do!" Peter responded.

Jesus said, "Then take care of My sheep."

He asked a third time and Peter insisted, "Lord, You know everything, You know that I love You."

"Then feed My sheep!" Jesus continued, "The truth is, when you were young, you went where you wanted and did as you wished. But when you're old, you will stretch out your hands, and others will bind you, and take you where you don't want to go." He said this to let Peter know by what kind of death he would bring glory to God.

Peter noticed John behind them and asked, "And what about him Lord, what sort of death will he have?"

Jesus answered, "If I want him to remain until I return, what is that to you. You follow Me."

He said to all eleven, "I have been given all power and authority in heaven and on earth. Therefore, go and make disciples of all peoples, baptizing them in the name of the Father, and of the Son, and of the Holy Spirit. Those who believe and are baptized will be saved. Those who refuse to believe will be condemned. Teach them to obey all the commands I have given you. And believe that I am with you always, even to the end of the world."

Then Jesus led them to Bethany, and lifting His hands, He blessed them.

Having done this, He left them, and headed home to heaven.

Genealogy of Jesus Christ

This is the family history of Jesus Christ, the Messiah, from Abraham to Joseph - the husband of Mary - the mother of Jesus. Abraham was the father of Isaac; whose son was Jacob; whose son was Judah; whose son was Perez; whose son was Hezron; whose son was Ram; whose son was Amminadab; whose son was Nahshon; whose son was Salmon; whose son was Boaz; whose son was Obed; whose son was Jesse; whose son was King David; whose son was Solomon; whose son was Rehoboam; whose son was Abijah; whose son was Asa; whose son was Jehoshaphat; whose son was Jehoram; whose son was Uzziah; whose son was Jotham; whose son was Ahaz; whose son was Hezekiah; whose son was Manasseh; whose son was Amon; whose son was Josiah; whose son was Jeconiah; whose son was Shealtiel; whose son was Zerubbabel; whose son was Abiud; whose son was Eliakim; whose son was Azor; whose son was Zadok; whose son was Achim; whose son was Eliud; whose son was Eleazar; whose son was Matthan; whose son was Jacob; whose son was Joseph - the husband of Mary - the mother of Jesus.

Parables and Lessons to Learn By

Sermon on the Mount
Blessed are the poor in spirit, for the Kingdom of Heaven is theirs; Blessed are those who mourn, for they shall be comforted; Blessed are the humble, for they shall inherit the earth; Blessed are those who hunger and thirst for righteousness, for they shall be filled; Blessed are the merciful, for they shall be shown mercy; Blessed are the pure in heart, for they shall see God; Blessed are the peacemakers, for they shall be called children of God; Blessed are those who are persecuted because they live for God, for theirs is the Kingdom of Heaven.

Salt
You are the salt of the earth. But if salt has lost its flavor, how can it be made salty again? It will be thrown out and trampled underfoot.

Light
You are a light to the world, like a city on a hill which cannot be hidden. No one lights a lamp and puts it under a basket; but on a lamp stand, so that it shines for all who see it. Likewise, let your good deeds shine out for all to see; so that every one will praise your heavenly Father.

Law
I did not come to abolish the Law or the Prophets, but

to fulfill. Until heaven and earth pass away, not the least detail of God's Law will disappear before all is fulfilled. Those who break these commandments, and teach others to do so, shall be called least in the Kingdom of Heaven. Those who obey God's Laws, and teach them to others, will be called great in the Kingdom of Heaven.

Anger
You have heard it said, "You shall not commit murder." But I say to you that if you are even angry with someone, without just cause, you are in danger of judgment.

Offerings
If you bring your gift to the altar and there remember that someone has something against you, first go to that person and be reconciled. Then come and offer your gift. Settle matters with an adversary before he takes you to court, lest he hand you over to the authority and you find yourself in prison.

Adultery
The commandment has said, "You shall not commit adultery." But I say to you that a man who looks at a woman to lust after her, has already committed adultery in his heart. If your eye causes you to sin, remove it and throw it away. Better to lose one part of your body than to have your whole body cast into Hell fire. The same applies to other members of your body.

Divorce

It has been said that a man can divorce his wife by giving her a certificate of divorce. But I tell you that a man who divorces his wife, except for marital unfaithfulness, causes her to commit adultery; if she marries again. A man who marries a divorced woman also commits adultery.

Vows

Our ancestors were told, "You must not swear falsely; instead fulfill your vows made to the Lord." But I say that you should not swear an oath at all. Simply let your 'yes' be 'yes' and let your 'no' be 'no'. Your word should be enough.

Revenge

The law has said, "The punishment must match the injury; and eye for an eye and a tooth for a tooth." I would say instead that you should not retaliate. If someone tries to take your coat, give him your shirt also. If someone compels you to carry his burden one mile, go with him two miles. Give to the one who asks of you, and don't turn away from the one who wants to borrow from you.

Love

You have heard it said, "Love your neighbors and hate your enemies." But I say, love your enemies, and bless those who persecute you. Do good to those who hate you, that you may be children of your Father in heaven. He causes the sun to shine on the evil and on the good. He sends rain on both the just and the unjust. Strive to be perfect, as your Father in heaven is perfect.

Giving
Don't do your good deeds seeking admiration from men. If you do that, you already have your reward. Give in secret, and your Father who sees in secret, will reward you openly.

Prayer
When you pray, do it in your quiet place, and don't use vain repetitions. Pray something like this, "Father in heaven, may Your name always be kept holy. May Your Kingdom come and Your will be done, here on earth as it is in heaven. Give us our needs for this day, and forgive our sins, just as we forgive those who sin against us. Help us to not yield to temptation, and protect us from the evil one. Give us grace to forgive others; then we will know that You have forgiven us."

Fasting
When you fast, don't appear obvious, as the hypocrites do, for they will get no other reward. Wash your face and comb your hair; then only your Father in heaven will know you are fasting, and He will reward you.

Treasures
Don't accumulate treasures here on earth; where moths

and rust destroy, and thieves break in and steal. But lay up treasures in heaven where they are safe. For where your treasure is, there your heart will be also. Keep your sights on a heavenly goal for the eyes are a light for the body and, if your eyes are good, your whole body will be filled with light.

Judging
If you judge others, you too will be judged in the same way that you judge them. Why do you notice a speck in your friend's eye when you don't even consider the plank in your own eye? First remove the plank from your eye so you can see clearly to remove the speck from your friend's eye.

Effective Prayer
Keep on asking, and searching, and knocking and God will open doors for you. If your children ask for bread, will you give them a stone? Or if they ask for a fish, will you give them a snake? If sinful people know how to give good gifts to their children, how much more will your heavenly Father give good gifts to those who ask Him.

The Golden Rule
Do to others as you would want them to do to you. This command sums up the Law and the Prophets.

The Narrow Gate
The gate is wide and the road is easy that leads to

destruction, and many choose that way. The gate is narrow and the path difficult that leads to God's Kingdom, and there are few who find it.

Fruit

You will know God's children by their actions. Do men gather grapes from thorn bushes, or figs from thistles? A good tree bears good fruit and a bad tree bears bad fruit. Every tree that does not bear good fruit will be cut down and thrown into the fire.

True Disciples

Not all who say, 'Lord, Lord', will enter the Kingdom of Heaven. Only those who do the will of My Father who is in heaven. Many will say on that day, 'But Lord, we prophesied in Your name, and cast out demons in Your name, and performed miracles in Your name,' But I will reply, "I never knew you. Leave Me, you who break God's Laws."

Solid Rock

Whoever hears My words and obeys is like a man who built his house on solid rock. The winds blew and the flood waters came and beat against the house, but it stood firm because it had a solid foundation. Anyone who does not obey is like a man who built his house with no foundation at all. The winds blew and the flood waters came, and the house was gone.

Patches and Wineskins

No one sews a piece of unshrunk cloth on an old garment, for the new piece will shrink and pull away from the old, and the tear will be made worse. Also, no one puts new wine into old wineskins, for the new wine will burst the old wineskins and all will be ruined. New wine must be put into new wineskins.

Students

Students are not greater than their teacher; nor servants than their master. But students well taught, will become like their teacher.

Revelation

Don't fear those who can kill the body but cannot harm the soul; fear only God who can destroy both body and soul in Hell fire.

Sparrows

What is the price of two sparrows; one copper coin? Yet not one can fall to the ground without your Father's knowledge. He even knows the number of hairs on your head. Have faith then, for you are far more valuable to God than a whole flock of sparrows.

Sword

I have not come to bring peace to the earth; but a sword. I have come to set one family member against another, and your enemies will be those of your own household. If you love your father or mother more than Me, you are not worthy of Me. And if you will not take up your cross and follow Me, you are not worthy of Me. Whoever clings to his life will lose it, and whoever loses his life for My sake will find it.

A Good Heart

A good person speaks good things from a good heart, and a wicked person speaks wicked things from an evil heart. The words you speak can justify you, or they can condemn you.

The Sower

The message of God's Kingdom can be likened to a farmer who went out to sow seeds. Some fell on a footpath, and the birds came and ate them. These are those who hear the Word, but don't understand. Satan comes at once to steal away that which was sown. Some fell on shallow soil and, because they could find no depth to root, soon withered away. These are those who receive the Word with joy, but because they have no root, fall away when trials come. Some fell among thorn bushes, which soon choked the tender plants. These are those who hear the Word only to have it crowded out by other worries, cares, and pleasures of this life. Some fell on fertile ground and yielded a good crop. These are those who hear the Message, and understand it, and produce an abundant harvest.

Wheat and Weeds

The Kingdom of Heaven is like a man who sowed good seed in his field. While the servants slept, an enemy came and sowed weeds among the wheat. When the crop began to grow, the weeds also grew. The servants asked, "Sir, do you want us to pull out the weeds?" "No!" He replied, "You'll uproot the wheat if you do. Let them grow together until the harvest. Then I will tell the harvesters to sort out the weeds, tie them in bundles and burn them. But gather the wheat into my barn." The sower of the good seed is the Son of Man. The field is the world. The good seeds are those who belong to God. The sower of weeds is Satan. The weeds are those who belong to Satan. The harvest is the end of the age. The harvesters are the angels.

Mustard Seed
The Kingdom of Heaven is like a tiny mustard seed. When it is sown, it grows large and birds come to nest in its branches, and to rest in its shade.

Yeast
The Kingdom of Heaven is like the small amount of yeast a woman uses in making bread. Soon all the dough has risen.

Treasure
The Kingdom of Heaven is like treasure which a man found hidden in a field. In his joy, he hid it again and went and sold all he had, and bought the field.

Fishing Net

The Kingdom of Heaven is like a fishing net that was lowered into the water, and caught fish of every kind. When on shore, the good fish were sorted into special containers, and the bad were thrown away. That's how it will be at the end of the age. The righteous will be separated to God. The wicked will be cast into everlasting fire, where there will be weeping and gnashing of teeth.

Little Children

Unless you turn from your sins and become like little children, you will never enter the Kingdom of Heaven. Whoever receives a little child in My name receives Me. But anyone who causes one of these little ones who believe in Me to fall into sin, it would be better for him to have a large stone chained to his neck, and be drowned in the depths of the sea.

Lost Sheep

If a shepherd has a hundred sheep, and one is lost, won't he leave the ninety-nine, and go and search for the one that is lost? When he finds it, he will rejoice over that one more than all the others that didn't wander off. In the same way, the Father's will is that none of His little ones should perish.

Correcting a Brother

If a brother sins against you, go to him privately and point out his offence. If he listens and confesses it, you have won your brother back. If he refuses to listen go again, but take one or two others with you, so that all you say may be confirmed by two or three witnesses. If he still refuses to listen, tell it to the church and if he refuses even the church, let him be as a heathen to you.

The Unforgiving Debtor

The Kingdom of Heaven is like a certain King who chose to settle accounts with his servants. One was brought in who owed a great deal of money which he was not able to pay. So the King ordered that his family and all that he had be sold to pay the debt. The servant pleaded, "Please, be patient with me and I will pay in full." The King was moved with compassion and forgave the entire debt. Later that servant found a fellow servant who owed him a very small amount of money. He grabbed his fellow servant and demanded instant payment. The other servant pleaded, "Have patience with me and I will pay it all." But he wouldn't wait. He had his debtor thrown in prison until the debt would be paid in full. This upset other servants who told the King, and the man was called back in, "You wicked servant!" The King said, "I forgave your tremendous debt because you pleaded with me. Shouldn't you likewise have shown mercy to your fellow servant?" The angry King handed the wicked servant over to the jailers, until he paid back all that he owed.

The Landowner

The Kingdom of Heaven is like a landowner who went out early one morning to hire laborers for his vineyard. They agreed on one denarius, which was the normal day's wage, and went to work. Later, he saw others standing idle and told them, "Go into my vineyard, and I will pay you whatever is right." A few hours later and then again still later, he saw others doing nothing and said to them, "You also go to my vineyard, and I will pay you whatever is right." When evening came, the owner said to his manager, "Call in the laborers and give them their wages, beginning with the last to the first." Those who had only worked one hour each received one denarius. When those who had worked all day also received one denarius each, they complained, "These last men have worked only one hour and you've made them equal to us who have borne the burden and the heat of the day." The owner answered, "Friend, I've done you no wrong. Didn't we agree on one denarius? Can't I do as I wish with my money? Don't you know that the last will be first, and the first last, for many are called, but few are chosen."

Two Sons

Consider this! A man with two sons told the older one, "Son, go out and work in the vineyard today." The boy answered, "No, I won't go!" But later he changed his mind and went. To his younger son he said the same, and the boy replied, "I will go, Sir." But he did not go. Which of the two obeyed his father? Wasn't it the first?

Wicked Renters

A landowner planted a vineyard and set a hedge around it. He dug a winepress and built a lookout tower. Then he rented the vineyard to tenants and left on a long journey. When the harvest time came, he sent servants to collect his share of the crop. But the vinedressers caught the servants and beat one, killed one, and stoned another. So the owner sent more servants and the tenants did likewise to them. Last of all he sent his son saying, "Surely they will respect my son." When the tenants saw the son, they plotted, "This is the heir. We'll kill him and seize his inheritance." When the owner returns, will he not destroy those wicked renters, and lease the vineyard to others who will do right by him?

Wedding Feast

The Kingdom of Heaven is like a King who prepared a great wedding feast for his son. When all was ready, he sent servants to call in all those who had been invited, but they refused to come. Then he sent more servants, urging them, "Come now, for all is ready!" The invited ones ignored them; some going to their fields, some to their business, and some seized the servants and mistreated them badly; even killing some. When the King heard this he was enraged and ordered his army to destroy both them and their city. To his other servants he said, "The feast is ready, but those who were invited were not worthy. Go into the streets and the hedges and bring in everyone you find, that the banquet hall may be filled." When the King came into greet the guests, he noticed a man who had refused to put on the wedding garment, which the host provides. He said, "Friend, why did you come in here without a wedding garment?" Then he ordered the man bound hand and foot, and cast out into the outer darkness, where there will be weeping and gnashing of teeth. For many are called, but few are chosen.

God First
"Hear Oh Israel, the Lord is God, the Lord is one. You shall love the Lord your God with all your heart, with all your soul, with all your mind, and with all your strength. This is the first and greatest commandment. The second is like it, you shall love your neighbor as yourself. This is the essence of the Law and the Prophets."

Ten Bridesmaids
In that day, the Kingdom of Heaven will be like ten bridesmaids, who took their lamps and went out to meet the bridegroom. Five were foolish and took only their lamps with only a little oil. Five were wise and brought along extra oil for their lamps. When the bridegroom was delayed, they all grew tired and laid down and slept. About midnight, a cry rang out, "The bridegroom is coming, come out to meet him!" The bridesmaids awoke and trimmed their lamps. The foolish said to the wise, "Give us some of your oil for

our lamps are going out." The wise replied, "No! We don't have enough to share with you. Go to those who sell and buy some for yourselves." While the foolish were gone, the bridegroom arrived, and the wise went in with him to the marriage feast, and the door was locked. When the foolish returned, they called from outside, "Lord, open the door for us!" But he called back, "Believe Me when I say that I don't know you." The moral is 'Stay Alert', for you do not know the day nor the hour of His return.

Three Servants

The Kingdom of Heaven is like a man traveling to a far country, who entrusted his money to his servants in his absence. To one he gave five talents, to one two talents, and to one he gave one talent. After some time, the master returned and asked the servants to give account of how they had used his money. The first said, "Master, you gave me five talents. I have invested it and earned five more." Likewise, the second said, "Master, you gave me two talents. I have put it to work and gained two more." The Master said, "Well done, good and faithful servants. You have been wise in handling small things, now I will put you in charge of greater things." The servant with one talent said, "Master, I know you are a harsh man, often reaping where you didn't cultivate. I was afraid I might lose your money, so I hid it, but here it is." The master replied, "You foolish and lazy servant. You know that I am a hard man. You should have at least deposited my money with the bankers so that I would have gained some interest on it. Now give the talent you have to the one who has ten. For to those who use well what they are given, even more will be given. But to the foolish, even what little they have will be taken away." To the other servants he said, "Throw this one out into the outer darkness where there will be weeping and gnashing of teeth."

Lost Coin

Suppose a woman has ten valuable coins and loses one. Will she not light a lamp, sweep the house, and search carefully until she finds it? Then she calls friends and neighbors and says, "Rejoice with me, for I have found my lost coin." In the same way, there is rejoicing in the presence of God's angels when even one sinner repents.

Lost Son

A man had two sons. The younger said to his father, "Give me my inheritance now, before you die." His father divided his share to him and he left, with all his belongings for a distant land where he squandered all he had in wild living. A famine swept over the land, and he was starving. A local farmer hired him and sent him into the fields to feed pigs. He was so hungry that even what the pigs were eating looked good to him. When he came to his senses he thought, "At home, even the hired servants have plenty to eat, and yet here I am starving. I will go to my father and tell him that I have sinned against heaven and against him, and that I am not worthy to be called his son. But if he will just let me be as one of the hired servants, I will have food to eat." While he was still a long way off, his father saw him coming. Overcome with love and compassion, he ran to his son, threw his arms around him and kissed him. "Quick!" He told the servants, "Bring the best robe and put it on him. Put a ring on his finger and sandals on his feet. Kill the fatted calf and let's celebrate, for my son who was dead is alive again. The older son was coming in from the fields when he heard music and laughter coming from the house. He asked a servant what the cause of this celebration was. The servant answered, "Your brother has come home, and it is a joyous occasion." The older son was angry and would not go in, so his father came out and pleaded with him. But he said, "All these years I've slaved for you, and have never once failed to do what you've asked. Yet you have never given me even one small goat so I could celebrate with my friends. And then when he shows up, you treat him like royalty." His father said, "My son, you are always with me and everything I have is yours. But your brother, who was dead to us, is alive again. What was lost has been found, and this is reason to celebrate."

Shrewd Manager

A certain rich man had a manager, who was accused of wasting his employer's money. When called to account, the manager was told "Get your report in order because you are going to be fired." The manager thought, "What will I do? I'm not strong enough to dig, and I would be too ashamed to beg. I know what I'll do so that people will welcome me into their homes when I've lost my job." So he called in all of his employer's debtors. To one he said, 'How much do you owe?" The man answered, "One hundred measures of oil." The manager replied, "Take your bill and change it to fifty." To another he said, "How much do you owe?" The man answered, "One hundred measures of wheat." The manager told him, "Take your bill and write eighty." The employer was impressed with the dishonest manager because he had acted shrewdly. The lesson is this: Use your worldly resources to benefit others and to make friends. Then when your earthly treasures are gone, you will be welcomed into an eternal home.

Lazarus and the Rich Man

There was a rich man, who dressed in purple and fine linen, and who lived in luxury every day. At his gate lay Lazarus, a beggar covered with sores so that the dogs came and licked at him. Lazarus longed for scraps from the rich man's table, but was given none. In time he died, and was carried by angels to Abraham's side. The rich man died also but he, in torment, saw Abraham in the distance with Lazarus at his side. He called, "Father Abraham, send Lazarus to dip his finger in water, then come and cool my tongue, for I am in terrible agony." Abraham said, "Remember in your life, you had everything you wanted, but Lazarus had nothing. Now, here he is comforted, while you are suffering. Besides, a great chasm

separates us so that neither we nor you can cross over."
The rich man pleaded, "Please father Abraham, at least send him to my father's house for I have five brothers. He can warn them so that they don't end up here." Abraham replied, "They have been warned by Moses and the Prophets. If they won't listen to them, even someone coming back from the dead will not persuade them."

Mustard Seed Faith
If you have faith even though it be as small as a mustard seed, you can say to this mulberry tree, "Be uprooted and planted in the sea," and it will obey you.

The Good Shepherd
He is a thief and a robber, who tries to enter the sheepfold by any other way except through the gate. The shepherd enters by the gate. He calls his sheep by name, and they come to him because they know his voice. They will follow him willingly, but will run from a stranger, whose voice they do not know.

The Good Samaritan
A man was traveling from Jerusalem to Jericho, when he fell among thieves. They took his clothes and money, then beat him and left him badly wounded. A priest came along but, seeing the wounded man, he crossed the road and passed on the other side. A Levite saw him, and also passed on the other side. But when a Samaritan came by, he had compassion on the man, and soothed his wounds with olive oil and wine,

and bandaged them. Then he helped the man onto his own animal, and brought him to an Inn, and took care of him. He handed some coins to the Innkeeper and told him, "Look after this man, and if it costs more, I'll repay you when I pass this way again." Who was a neighbor to the man? Isn't it the one who showed mercy?

The Rich Fool

A rich man had many acres of fertile ground that produced abundant harvests. "What should I do?" He thought, "I don't have room to store all my crops. I know, I'll tear down my barns and build bigger ones. Then I'll have enough stored away for years to come. I can take life easy; eat, drink, and relax." But God said to him, "Fool! What if you die this very night? Then who will benefit from everything you've worked for? This is how it will be for those who store up earthly treasures, but are not rich toward God."

The Pharisee and the Tax Collector

Two men went to the temple to pray, one a Pharisee and the other a tax collector. The Pharisee stood proud and prayed, "Thank God that I'm not like these other men. I don't cheat, I don't steal, and I don't commit adultery. I fast twice a week and tithe a tenth of all I get." But the tax collector knelt at a distance and dared not even lift his eyes to heaven as he prayed. Instead, he beat his chest in sorrow praying, "Oh God, have mercy on me, for I am a sinner." Which one left justified? Those who exalt themselves will be humbled, and those who humble themselves will be exalted.

Final Judgment

When Jesus comes in His glory, and all His angels with Him, then He will sit on His glorious throne. All peoples will be gathered before Him. He will separate them, as a shepherd separates the sheep from the goats. The believers will be at His right hand, and the unbelievers will be at His left. He will say to those on His right, "Come, you who are blessed of My Father, and inherit the Kingdom prepared for you from the creation of the world. For I was hungry, and you gave Me food. I was thirsty and you gave Me drink. I was a stranger and you took Me in. I needed clothing, and you clothed Me. I was sick, and you cared for Me. I was in prison, and you came to visit Me." The righteous will ask, "Lord, when did we ever see You hungry, or thirsty, or a stranger, or naked, or sick, or in prison, and minister to Your needs?" The Lord will answer, "When you met the needs of others, you were doing it to Me." He will then say to the unrighteous, "Depart from Me, you who are cursed, into the eternal fire prepared for the Devil and his angels. For you shunned Me when I was in need, and you didn't visit Me when I was confined. You have earned your reward."

Money and Possessions

No one can serve two Masters. For either he will hate the one and love the other, or else he will be loyal to the one and despise the other. You cannot serve God and money. Don't worry about your life, what you will eat or drink; or about your body, what you will wear. Isn't life more important than food, and your body more than clothing? Consider the birds. They don't plant, nor harvest, nor gather into barns, yet your heavenly Father feeds them. Aren't you more valuable to Him than they are? And why worry about clothing. See how the lilies of the field grow. They don't labor or worry, and yet, even   Solomon in all his glory was not clothed as elegantly as one of these. Aren't you more important to God than lilies? So don't worry. Your heavenly Father   already knows your needs. Seek His Kingdom first, and live righteously, and He will give you what you need. And remember, "No one can serve both God and money."

The
Combined
Gospel

What does Jesus have for you?

Have you ever come across a deal that seems far too good to be true? This one is true, and very real; and free. There is nothing you can do to earn it, and no amount of money with which you could ever buy it. Ephesians 2: 8-9 tells us that the salvation God offers us is is a gift, completely free of charge. However, even gift will never be ours if we won't accept it. Romans 3:23 tells us that all have sinned and fall short of the glory of God. All are under sins curse. If that were not so, we wouldn't be subject to death. We all need a Savior. We all need Jesus. He died an awful death and thereby paid the impossible debt that we owed, so that we can have the chance to spend a glorious, never-ending eternity with Him. And all it takes is an honest, sincere little talk with Him. Accept His gift. Admit to Him that you are a sinner and you need Him to forgive you. Ask Him to enter your heart and your life and fill that emptiness which only He can fill. What can it hurt? Believe in Him; talk to Him; invite Him in; and love Him.